MINDFUL
WALKING

WALK YOUR WAY TO
MENTAL AND PHYSICAL
WELL-BEING

Hugh O'Donovan, Reg Psychol, PsSI, MISCP, MBPsS, is a registered psychologist (work), performance coach and former army officer. Hugh has a passionate interest in and commitment to applying the best-practise, evidence-based insights of psychology (positive), coaching psychology and contemplative neuroscience, in order to enhance the life experience, work performance and well-being of individuals, groups and organisations.

Co-Founder of the first Master's in Coaching Psychology to be delivered in an Irish university (UCC) and Programme Co-Director on the Higher Diploma in Coaching/Coaching Psychology, also in UCC, Hugh is, in addition, honorary Vice-President of the International Society for Coaching Psychology.

He lives in Cork with his wife Michele and his daughters Aoife and Jean. In his spare time, he likes to cook, trek to high, remote places, enjoy good company and explore archaeological artefacts, preferably all at the one time.

MINDFUL WALKING

WALK YOUR WAY TO MENTAL AND PHYSICAL WELL-BEING

HUGH O'DONOVAN

HACHETTE
BOOKS
IRELAND

First published in 2015 by Hachette Books Ireland
First published in paperback in 2015
A division of Hachette UK Ltd.

Copyright © Hugh O'Donovan 2015

A CIP catalogue record for this title is available from the British Library.

ISBN 978 1473 613 898

Cover design, typeset and layout design by redrattledesign.com

Illustration used with kind permission of Walter Quirke

Printed and bound by CPI Group (UK) Ltd, Croydon, CR0 4YY

Some of the names and details in this book have been changed to protect
the privacy of individuals

Hachette Books Ireland policy is to use papers that are natural, renewable
and recyclable products and made from wood grown in sustainable forests.
The logging and manufacturing processes are expected to conform to the
environmental regulations of the country of origin.

Hachette Books Ireland
8 Castlecourt Centre
Castleknock
Dublin 15
Ireland

A division of Hachette UK Ltd
Carmelite House
50 Victoria Embankment
London EC47 0DZ

www.hachette.ie

To my friend, my partner, my rock,
my wife Michele

CONTENTS

MINDFUL WALKING: WALK YOUR WAY TO MENTAL AND PHYSICAL WELL-BEING

INTRODUCTION

Can you remember a time when you didn't walk? Or imagine a time when you won't walk? In a lifetime you could walk 150,000 miles – about 10,000 steps a day adding up to about 5 miles a day, or 8 kilometres, over 80 years. You may well take walking for granted. You always had to walk to carry the day forward, whether marching to and from school, being exhorted on family walks, or escaping the office for some fresh air at lunch. You have certainly walked in many places but have you appreciated the benefits to your mind and body which walking has given you? Can you sense how much greater those benefits would be if you walked mindfully, with intention, focus and attitude? If you opened your eyes and wandered with curiosity, in the moment? Mindful walking is the special place where mind, body, people and the natural environment come together. It is a place of well-being, a place where you feel alive.

In a busy life we spend much of our time juggling tasks, solving problems and balancing demands. We can bob like corks on what seems like a sea of endless challenge and change, and get tossed about the choppy waves. We can feel tense, tired, drained and empty. Our minds and bodies can be complicit in all of this. The way we think and its impact on our wider nervous system play a central part in how we engage with the challenges we face in life and our unfolding experience. Is there a better way to live our lives? The evidence suggests that yes, there is.

When people pick up a book like this they are often looking to find their way through a difficult time. Many people want to choose their own path and be their own agents of change, learning new approaches and exploring new territory. In my work as a coaching psychologist I meet all kinds of people, from stay-home parents to senior executives, students and business owners. I sometimes refer to this wide spectrum of people as the 'worried well.'

The 'worried well' might be functioning well in their everyday lives, but something doesn't feel right. They are not inured from the anxiety, fear and lowness which impacts on our well-being and happiness. They are often searching for something they cannot define. I often talk to people about three possible paths to take. These are paths that can change the way we live our lives. Each one can transform our mood, improve our wellness and set us on a different course. Put all three together from time to time and you can walk mindfully to a better place.

1. Talk

We can always talk through our challenges and worries. The power of informal talking with friends is not to be underestimated. Life can be debated, new possibilities considered and fun had. Creating a structured space where we feel safe to talk is also important, and much psychological research underpins the efficacy of talking therapies.

2. Meditate

Ancient Eastern philosophers wrote about the dangers of the wandering, judgemental mind. It is a mind that can work in error, bias and distortion for us all. Eastern traditions offer us a strategy to train that mind. The emergence of mindfulness in the 21st century into the wider public consciousness in the West seems to point to its need at this time. Mindfulness is no longer an esoteric practise, it is a shared way of life, and its benefits are increasingly evidence-based. This evidence is an added comfort for people who are sceptical of alternative thinking; the science of mindfulness connects us with the older wisdom of meditation. Mindfulness increasingly makes sense.

3. Walk

Movement is intrinsic to being human, and has been since our first ancestors roamed the earth six million years ago. We were made to move: the initial reason for a brain and a nervous system was to either promote or suppress movement, and our ability to think and reason came much later in our evolutionary story. But we are increasingly more sedentary. Gentle mindful movement gets mind and body working together like an orchestra. It enhances life experience, health and well-being. You are the conductor. No one is going to take you from your own path.

Mindful walking joins these three paths together and awakens us to our full potential in life. We know that we need to walk more, talk more, and focus more from time to time. With mindful walking, we can also set and take on challenges beyond our comfort zone.

It is a curious benefit of movement that people tend to talk very openly and personally when walking. Walking sheds away the casing of reserve that clings to us in our everyday exchanges. When people walk together in nature, on the beach or on the mountain, this opening up happens with even greater ease – you must have noticed this too. As someone remarked to me recently, you feel drunk without having to wake up to the aching head and embarrassing memories of a hangover. Drinking is an efficient way to deaden our pain but usually overnight that pain comes back to haunt us. A mindful approach to life is not about deadening the mind or the senses. It is about accepting our pain and walking with it, and accepting our aliveness. The magic of being alive doesn't need extra stimulants to be felt. With mindful walking that magical sense can come from within, through our own movement and experience of nature. We feel highs, but only ones we come down from gently, and there is no blurry aftermath to face. Mindfulness brings joy without addiction.

You might be aware that in meditation, there are four traditional postures: sitting, lying, standing and walking. In this book I am going to expand the walking posture to explore the various contexts of mindful walking, at home, in gardens or parks, through city streets, across wild landscapes and even upon the highest peaks of the world. Mindful walking means walking with a deliberate intention, focus and attitude. It is noticing without attachment, as best we can, our unfolding experience in an open, curious and non-judgemental way. On a mindful walk we don't judge ourselves or others. We stand back from our reactions, and respond gently to what comes our way. And as we'll see, we can integrate this into our daily lives. We can walk mindfully in metres or kilometres, on a remote trail or through the high streets of a city, breathing in the buzz of life.

Mindful walking is a gentle and compassionate way to take full responsibility for the only thing that you can take full responsibility for – yourself. Awakening to your inner authentic energy and potential is a wonderful new journey of possibility. This is not to say that the way is smooth or easy. There will of course be obstacles and potholes along the road. It is not in any way to paint a romantic version of sunshine moments. The rain runs down the back of the neck on occasions but that can also be experienced mindfully too. My hope is that in reading this book, you will find your footing, and capture a way to walk mindfully to places you never imagined you would go.

The simple yet powerful act of walking into your future now begins. Why not stand up now. Then take a step. It is a positive statement of intent.

Keep a Diary

One special way of capturing the essence of your mindful walking practise and even wider consciousness is to open a diary as you experiment with this new way of moving and noticing. As you set out to read this book and begin your mindfulness practise in earnest, reflecting from time to time on your thinking and emotions and behaviours and actually capturing it in writing in a diary is a powerful way to see how you are really thinking and feeling and behaving. It is a way of speaking to yourself in the present moment. In a curious way writing fits with walking because it is a mind/body thing. Mind and body movement are linked.

Diarying is just capturing what is on our minds and expressing out into the world whatever challenges, fears, anxieties or excitement we are noticing and experiencing. Over time we can begin to notice patterns to our own engagement with life that may be unmindful and unhelpful. It could even be the makings of your first book.

TAKE THE STAIRS

To learn something new is to get to know yourself. In the process of learning about who you are, your desires and your struggles, you are likely to discover what may bring well-being, happiness and peace to your life. In walking mindfully with curiosity you can have many new experiences. You will certainly meet new people and see new places beyond your current reckoning. Don't be afraid! You will be your own agent, and set the pace yourself. You will have time to reflect on what you have achieved, and bring a new hope and meaning to the future that will serve you well.

The benefits of walking are increasingly being promoted by governments and authorities as a means of improving public health. Diseases such as cancer, obesity, heart disease and diabetes are being targeted through regular walking programmes. But there are inconvenient truths. The World Health Organisation says that physical inactivity is currently the fourth largest contributor to global death. For some time now, the WHO has recommended adults to undertake moderate-intensity aerobic walking amounting to 30 minutes a day, 5 days per week. However, only one third of adults reach this goal. We must walk together to correct this shortfall.

The well-known '20 Plus Campaign' recommends per day 20 seconds of intense activity (such as running up stairs), a minimum of 20 minutes of walking and no more than 20 minutes sitting at any one time. While medical opinions differ on the lengths and strengths, no health practitioner disagrees with the contention that the need to get up and move around is essential to our well-being. We are not designed to be sedentary. You know the ways you can creatively incorporate walking into your own life. It makes sense to walk instead of sitting in a car, edging along in traffic. To walk up the stairs at work and feel your heartbeat rise, instead of twiddling your thumbs in an elevator. To walk out to lunch instead of eating 'al desco.' To walk into town, instead of waiting for a bus to take you only a few stops. It all adds up.

Experts in the field of psychology have shown that walking in natural settings is especially beneficial to our mental health. Robust studies show that short but frequent nature walks not only lift our mood but improve overall well-being. Walking in the countryside, in clean air, through forests, across streams and around lakes allows a powerful connection with the universe around us. As our enjoyment is enhanced, our intrinsic fascination with the world around us is piqued.

Children have this fascination when they walk and run about, stopping every few moments to pick up a leaf or an acorn, to study its design. As children, to be outside was to be carefree and in the moment. We must recover some of the skills of just being there in that moment of curiosity and learning. Once we adults regain this interest, we can develop the greater sensory awareness that is associated with mindfulness. We can gain more positive mental and emotional states and lower depression and stress levels.

Later in the book we will explore the benefits of walking alone and in groups in various settings, from noisy urban streets to your local farmer's field where mushrooms grow, and even to the highest peaks of Mount Kilimanjaro. Let us be reminded as we set off that walking is free. It carries a low risk of injury. It's gentle on the joints, and you can be assured you'll have your knees in years to come (which isn't always guaranteed to joggers or other athletes). Walking is a readily accessible way to improved health.

TO DO OR NOT TO DO

In exploring the concept of mindful walking, it is helpful to make a distinction between the mind states of 'doing' and 'being.' For many of us, the exclusive focus in our lives is on 'doing.' 'Doing' is rather frantic. It is about ambition, wanting, consuming, getting results, outcomes and achievements. We can fail to notice the potential physical and emotional consequences of all of this 'doing' for our health and well-being. We can overwork in pursuit of what we consider important to our sense of achievement and self-worth. The alternative is that routineness, monotony and boredom can creep in and also leech our energy from us. We struggle for the things we think will make us happy. If we don't get them, we long after them. We usually get them, only to wonder what it was all about.

The mind state of 'being', on the other hand, is about the need for safety, connectedness, contentment, reflection and relaxation. 'Being' is a more nurturing, generous mind state. It gives mind and body a chance to recover, regenerate and be at peace.

We live in a fragmented, chaotic and over-stimulating world. The madness of all the activity around us is that while we sit, sedentary, in front of the TV or tablet, we are being promised a perfect future. Are we living this future vicariously, sitting watching other people on a screen, or scrolling through words and images? We are being urged to earn more, to have more, to consume more. But even if we have everything in material terms, the newness of things loses its lustre very quickly. The world we face is changing at a rate that challenges our individual ability to adapt. Learning – or simply remembering – effective ways of adapting to these changes is important. Walking needs to borrow from your time. You need to lease a little of your time to walking. You would be surprised at how little time can actually be involved.

When we are struggling with something, it's easy to forget that each one of us struggles in life too. It's not just ourselves. Even when we are doing fine, we regularly vacate our experience. Sometimes we find ourselves sleepwalking through life, operating on autopilot. This is how the mind works to cope with adversity. There is a value in this autopilot mechanism, but it can be complicit in many of our problems. Isn't it remarkable that in all the information we accumulate every day, we don't have much awareness of our own inner, unfolding experience? The psychologists Matthew Killingsworth and Dan Gilbert of Harvard University argue in their research paper published in 2010 that 47 per cent of the time, our mind is off wandering. They also go on to suggest that 'unlike other animals, human beings spend a lot of time thinking about what is not going on around them, contemplating events that happened in the past, might happen in the future, or will never happen at all.' We have somewhere between 12,000 and 50,000 thoughts a day, most of which are self-directed and concerned with the same issues, moment to moment. Imagine these thoughts rotating on a grill, slow cooking. Of course we are going to overheat sometimes. Of course this happens to the person sitting next to us too.

We rush through activities and find it difficult to stay focused. We encounter obstacles that run counter to our wishes and sense of entitlement. We react instantaneously. We are preoccupied with the past or the future. We may experience emotions we are not fully aware of until later. Just like when we feel shocked after a fall, and only later feel the aches and pains, we may not notice the build-up of physical tension in our body until we experience pain. And through all this, we walk quickly from place to place without paying much attention to what, or who, we pass along the way. In our headlong rush to stay on top of things we at best miss a lot. At worst, we complicate and hide matters to a degree which causes us needless pain and suffering. This suffering can be avoided. With greater awareness, we can recognise our stress and the fact that we are overwhelmed.

As will hopefully become apparent in these pages, there is in fact no real difference between doing and being when we mindfully engage with our lives. Mindful 'doing' and 'being' can become one and a way of life. We can become less self-centred. We can become more alive and present to our unfolding experience, and lose that sense of entitlement that makes us hunger for the things we think make us happy. We can lose our attachment to the beliefs we hold and the outcomes we crave. We are more at ease with ourselves and the world. We are more effective and we perform better. Mindful walking is in fact a meditation that brings this 'doing' and 'being' together in a very natural, easy and balanced way. Mind and body are one.

'We don't see the world as it is,
we see it as we are.' Anaïs Nin

THE ANSWER AT YOUR FEET

Existence is a wonderful and magical thing. It belongs to us. We might sleepwalk through much of our lives, but for better or worse we do it in our own unique way. Nobody else does it like we do. Even when we are more present to our experience, good or bad, the beliefs we have about how the world works and the rules we follow may be holding us back from the full enjoyment and experience of life.

Beginning this exploration of mindfulness allows us the opportunity to understand ourselves and the direction we wish to take our lives. This goes beyond the negative perceptions of ourselves that may be holding us back. This is to build confidence where it is lacking and resilience where it is needed. Whether you are going through a tough time personally, are experiencing grief or loss of any sort, have become unemployed, are experiencing relationship difficulties or are just plain stuck, imagine now a way of:

- Controlling your emotions in a calmer, more responsive and measured manner;

- Making better decisions;

- Improving your memory and creativity;

- Dealing better with insomnia;

- Managing your stress;

- Coping with anxiety or mild depression;

- Boosting your immune system;

- Reducing your blood pressure;

- Managing your pain;

- Improving your physical fitness and energy.

Mindful walking has all this to offer. Mindful walking is about taking the first steps on a journey to a place of balance and aliveness that should be all too familiar to you, but maybe it isn't. Mindful walking is a practise wherein mind, body and a wider social context come together. The answer is at your feet, before your very eyes, in front of your nose. This is an invitation to walk and notice these things in a new way. In developing the practise of mindfulness and mindful walking you will hopefully come to a better understanding of yourself. You may have to change. The world certainly won't. It is going along its merry way in spite of us.

In this book you will be invited to practise and experience mindfulness both formally and informally in a number of postures and different contexts. Formal mindfulness practise involves setting aside a time each day to meditate in silence, whether lying, sitting, standing or walking. Informal mindfulness practise is about bringing an awareness to the present moment and a noticing to all aspects of your life. There are myriad practises, such as mindful eating, drinking and walking, to mindful sex. While the main focus of this book is on the informal practise of walking mindfully wherever we find ourselves in life, you will learn things here that you can bring to other aspects of your life. Looking at the tenets of mindfulness is a necessary and essential starting point to gain the benefits of this informal walking practise.

As we go through the book, other people will share stories of their mindfulness practise and life experience with us, and I will contribute accounts of mindful walking that were life-changing for me. By offering a scientific framework of what we know about the mind you will hopefully learn, and learn to experiment more in your own way. But mindfulness is not a technique that can be taught. 'It must be caught,' as Michael Chaskalson writes in *The Mindful Workplace*. With mindfulness, you can catch yourself noticing at a deeper level beyond the cursory, unconscious and automatic. It is like when you notice that first snowflake of winter that lands on your jacket, perfect in the moment only to dissolve in the warmth and curiosity of your gaze.

'A journey of a thousand miles begins with one step.' Lao Tzu

My First Mindful Walk

Wherever you find yourself now, in the office, at home, or in town, you can focus and take a mindful walk. You don't need to go too far or for too long at this time. Maybe try a maximum of five to ten minutes out and back. This is about movement with a particular focus, intent and attitude.

Before you begin to walk and give your full attention to this exercise,

Slowing Down

Bring your attention to the rhythmic coming and going of your breath. The in-breath. The out-breath. As we go on to explore other mindfulness practises, the breath will be used as an anchor for focusing your attention. This is the first great learning of mindfulness. Wherever you find yourself, the only time that you are fully present in the now is when you are aware of your breath. Bring this slower sense of things to the walk you are about to undertake.

Noticing

As you stand, become aware of your feet in contact with your shoes and the ground. Feel the weight of your body down through your torso, legs, heels and toes. Gently move your neck, arms and shoulders. Bend your knees slightly.

Notice any stiffness, tension or other sensations in the body. Notice your mood now, positive or negative. Maybe make a mental note on a scale of one to ten, where one is poor and ten is very good. Now you are ready to begin the walk, normally and naturally. As you go, focus on each sense in turn.

Seeing

Focus now in more detail on what you are seeing around you. The people, the surroundings, the buildings. Look around. Look up. Notice the colours and the shades. The light and shadows. Welcome each new view as if you are seeing it for the first time. Periodically, bring your attention back to the breath. Become aware of any thoughts and judgements that are arising. Notice them coming and going with each step. Take time to stop if you wish to notice some aspect that captures your attention. Move on.

Hearing

Now focus on what you are hearing. What sounds, if any, are coming into your awareness? Are they distant or close? Perhaps people are talking. You hear the sounds of the city or the neighbourhood. Cars passing. Are you aware of your thoughts as the mind processes all of the information? Are they positive or negative or neutral? In all of this the mind will inevitably wander to the most interesting and obvious aspects of your surroundings. Make an effort to come back to the breathing from time to time and notice the body and its movement through this space that is so rich and interesting.

Smelling

Now focus and become aware of any smells and aromas that attract your attention. Can you describe the fragrance? Does it remind you of anything? Do the smells arouse any reactions in your body? Likes or dislikes? Are they making you hungry? Maybe it is lunch time and the body is sending some messages.

Touching

As you walk along, you might want to pick something up, or open a door. Are you aware of the exquisitely efficient and complex movement in the body as it prepares to do your bidding?

The poetry of the fingers and hand as it folds around the door handle. This is something that is so automatic normally that we fail to appreciate how wondrous it is. Being more mindful to the reality with an open and childlike curiosity is applied awareness in action.

Feeling

Again, in walking mindfully, how would you now describe your mood and emotion? What are you feeling? Can you place the feeling in your body? Is there any urgency creeping into the walk at any time? Is there any sense that maybe it is time to turn back? Notice if you are aware of new intentions which are arising in you now. The remainder of the day is perhaps calling. Now continue on your way to the end of your first short mindful walk.

Finishing

Before you return to whatever you must attend to for the rest of the day, focus your attention and notice where you are now. What are your thoughts now? How does your body feel now? How would you rate your mood now on the scale of one to ten? Has it changed? In walking as you did, what did you notice that was new?

Most of us spend too much time in our heads, over-thinking in unmindful ways. We ruminate about things that have passed and over which we have no control. We anxiously and sometimes fearfully predict a future that never comes. We rush towards pleasure, and chase what we perceive to be positive experiences. Understandably, we seek to avoid painful ones. In all of this we are rarely present to what is actually happening around and within us. Our emotions, both positive and negative, serve a useful purpose. They flag what is important to us in life. The consequences of developing a practise that brings you to the only moment you ever have could be profoundly important. Not only do you come to know that moment of experience better but you may also come to know yourself better.

The core contention of this book is that a holistic mind, body and social approach to well-being, happiness and peace is not only beneficial but also readily accessible. Mindful walking is an integrated mind and body, physical and mental fitness regime which is available to all who have the gift of walking, wherever we find

1

A CASE FOR MINDFUL WALKING

'Life is available only in the present. That is why we should walk in such a way that every step can bring us to the here and now.' Thich Nhat Hanh

MIND AND MINDFULNESS: THE SCENE AND THE SCIENCE

Mindfulness mental training has its roots in Buddhism. In Pali language, where we find the early Buddhist scriptures, the word mindfulness translates as mental development. Today it is a practise that draws from ancient Eastern traditions and develops next to the needs of modern society and culture. The mindfulness movement has a robust base in the Mindfulness-Based Stress Reduction (MBSR) programmes devised by Jon Kabat-Zinn in 1979 at the University of Massachusetts Medical School. Kabat- Zinn comes from a scientific perspective, while other important practitioners such as Thich Nhat Hanh come from a modern Buddhist religious perspective. The dedication of these figures has helped popularise mindfulness in the West, as mindfulness courses are becoming available across all age groups and in life and work settings. Mindfulness today finds a place in areas such as the healthcare services, corporate settings and education, the police and even the military.

Any case for mindful walking needs to be set firmly in the context of the current evidence for the efficacy of mindfulness. The last 40 years have seen the science of mindfulness emerge, with the proliferation of thousands of research papers on the subject. Having this support and underpinning from the academic community encourages the growth of the movement, and its popularity: a recent Google search for mindfulness threw up 26½ million hits.

Neuroscience is now focusing on mindfulness, with the emergence of a new hybrid field in the study of the brain, called contemplative neuroscience. This new field brings together a number of overlapping disciplines to explore the neurological, physiological, cognitive, behavioural and social elements of mindfulness meditation. It has been known for thousands of years that meditation has profound positive effects. The science, it appears, is now catching up.

There is a considerable body of evidence now available to point to the benefits of mindfulness training and practise, and in these opening chapters we will get a feel for those benefits. First, the science bit. Despite advances in neuroscience, there is a lot that we simply don't know about the brain. However, we do have a very good idea of the structure of the brain. For example, we can now observe the electrical impulses in that area of the brain called the amygdala which very rapidly triggers emotions and bodily reactions in the wider nervous system in response to perceived danger. This is the 'fight or flight' response we can feel when we are stressed or threatened.

Mindfulness can have an opposite, but equally powerful, effect in that it can activate the relaxation response in the brain / body and bring potentially negative emotions under control. Mindfulness practise can increase grey matter concentrations observed in brain areas connected with sustained attention, emotion regulation and perspective taking. This grey matter is also involved in sensory perception such as seeing and hearing, memory, emotions, speech, decision-making and self-control. When we focus in a mindful way, we become more rational, and we can feel a greater capacity to detach from the inner critic, that stream of internal commentary which can sometimes be very negative. Studies have shown that mindfulness can also lead to a more robust immune system, enhanced empathy and reduced levels of anxiety and depression. This emerging evidence base is flagging the way to greater well-being and happiness.

Mindfulness training appears to increase emotional intelligence. The pillars of this intelligence are self-awareness and interpersonal awareness, our ability to relate to one another. Evidence shows that mindfulness reduces stress and other deeper kinds of psychological distress.

In one study, US marines who underwent an eight-week MBSR course showed greater levels of cognitive control (meaning ability to switch between tasks and problem-solve), increased self-awareness, more situational awareness (knowing what's going on) and better emotional regulation (coping skills).

The UK National Institute for Health and Care Excellence (NICE) recommends mindfulness training as an intervention that will build effectiveness and resilience in workplaces.

The UK Mental Health Foundation's 'Be Mindful' report of 2010 suggests that people who are more mindful:

- Have less negative thoughts and are able to let them go when they arise;

- Have greater awareness, understanding and acceptance of their emotions and recover faster from bad moods;

- Are more in control and are less likely to exhibit defensive or aggressive behaviours when they feel threatened;

- Enjoy more satisfying relationships and are better able to deal with conflict in those relationships.

Name and Tame: A Three-Minute Meditation

Mindfulness is fundamentally about developing greater awareness. This is a short introductory meditation to develop that awareness.

Find a quiet place to sit on a straight-backed chair. If it works for you, don't sit into the chair supported by the back of it but rather sit forward, head back and in line with a straight back and spine, feet flat and in contact with the floor.

In that position, close your eyes and, as best you can, bring the focus of your attention to the natural ebb and flow of your breath in and out of your body. This is something you may have never done before – or you may have tried and given up, or maybe you're a Zen master. Notice the breath and sensations associated with your breath as it comes and goes. Is your breathing shallow? Can you notice any sensation in your nostrils? There is a lot going on. Adopting a mindful mind / body focus is to be with and observe whatever arises and comes into awareness without judging it as good or bad. You don't have to breathe in a special way. It is as it is, just notice it and maintain the focus as best you can.

Inevitably, as you may also notice, the mind will drift and wander off, perhaps to a judgement of some sort. 'This is nice. This is silly. This is hard.' Random thoughts and memories may arise. Some plans for the future may come to mind. As you notice whatever thought arises, just bring your attention back to the breath without judging the thought or yourself harshly. It is only a thought. It is not reality. The important thing is not to judge, but just to notice that the mind has wandered. Bring it back to the breath each time you notice.

After the three minutes (you might consider using a timer or a mindfulness app) open your eyes and come back to the place where you are sitting.

The object of this exercise is to begin to notice the mind and the workings of the body, in particular the breath. This process of focused attention on the breath is central to the practise of mindfulness. The breath very simply is the anchor, the mooring, the safe harbour we can return to any time we wish. Perhaps you might now turn to your diary briefly. Try to capture some of the thoughts that you had during this brief sitting meditation. Where did your mind wander to? Was it about a memory of some past experience or was it about some future or planned experience? In your diary try to pinpoint where the mind took you. This is the beginning of a different way of relating to your experience. It is to know the patterns of that experience, positive, negative and neutral, in a radical new way that is easy to access, with your intention and commitment.

WHERE WE'RE GOING WRONG

As the title of this book urges, mindful walking is about a journey to well-being, happiness and peace. Drawn from key psychological research, here are five elements of the human condition which can interfere with our willingness to embark on that journey.

1. Ego (the thinking mind)

This can be self-centred, absorbed and prone to negativity, bias and error;

2. Emotions

Like fish on a hook, we can get snagged in our negative thoughts, with negative emotions following;

3. Habituated behaviours

We can be sensitive, pessimistic and introverted by nature. Much of this is conditioned from what we have learned in early childhood. Where irrational thinking and emotions interact, unhelpful behaviours can follow;

4. Lack of movement

Inactivity is a silent killer. We are experiencing

an obesity crisis in the West. Even while engaging in physical activity, our minds are rarely focused on the job at hand. The mind can be distracted and disturbed easily – a flighty state the Buddhists call the 'monkey mind';

5. Lack of close relationships

In the human condition there is a tension between the need to be alone and to belong. Being connected and attuned to other people is what gives variety and meaning to life. It is central to our well-being and happiness. Because of our unmindful thinking and behaviours we can spend much of the time at war with ourselves and with others.

Having looked in basic terms at how the brain works, let us take a look at the way the mind works. In his 2011 book *Thinking, Fast and Slow* the Nobel Laureate Daniel Kahneman changed the way we understand our thinking. He describes fast and slow thinking and here I broaden his important theory of human reasoning to include mindfulness. 'Fast' thinking is unconscious, automatic thinking and processing, where messages outside of awareness are being transmitted back and forth between the brain and body. This process efficiently manages our mental and physical energy when, for example, you're driving your car. You are not thinking about every single movement involved in changing a gear. The hand moves unconsciously and outside of awareness for the most part. Such automatic processing preserves energy for emergencies and for really critical tasks. Brain and body are always on the lookout and scanning the environment for threat; fear has been at the root of our psyche since the Stone Age.

'Slow' thinking is deliberate, conceptual, focused planning, problem-solving, results-based thinking, and action also resides here. Often our formal schooling is exclusively focused on this critical, analytical, measuring thinking style – slow thinking is about knowing how to think and act. As I write these words, this system of thinking is fully activated but I'm beginning to notice my energy levels dropping, as I have been writing for some time. This system can, when we are totally absorbed and interested in something, lead to a 'flow' state. I'm not quite in it myself at this moment in time, but you may have experienced that white heat of creativity when working on something you love. Time seems to stand still. We can become mentally and physically tired from this style of thinking and associated action. We need to manage this too. How do we do this? Well, mindfulness points the way.

I would add a third process, which is important to understanding mindfulness and mindful walking and the relationship to fast and slow thinking.

This system of non-thinking is mindfulness in action. It is a conscious observing, noticing, non-judging, patient, curious, accepting, trusting, non-striving and detached style of being with our unfolding mental and physical experience. Mindfulness is an observing process. Many of us have difficulty with this idea because of a lifelong conditioning that urges us to judge what is around us and think our way out of situations. Mindfulness involves allowing greater awareness of the underlying, unconscious, positive, negative and neutral drivers of our fast thinking. In that space of mindful awareness we also deliberately let go of the critical judging faculties of slow thinking and come into the now.

Fast and slow thinking are both designed to solve problems and keep us safe in the world. Throughout this book I will use the phrase 'conceptual mind.' Our conceptual, thinking mind comprises fast and slow thinking. For all the power of these modes of thinking to remember the past and envision the future, they are prone to error, bias and distortion. Mindfulness is more about 'whether to think' than 'what to think.' It presents us with choice. It is gentle and compassionate on the self, the world and those in it, and demands nothing except our full presence in the now. It is a place that allows us to respond more appropriately to what flies at us. It is a place where we can be both alert and calm.

Mindfulness is far from easy in practise, as it seeks to be at ease while the other busy 'doing' systems of mind continue as they are. It is however profoundly important that we develop the observational skills of asking ourselves whether to think. Returning to mindfulness, which is non-thinking, can battle-harden us for the times when fast and slow thinking become overwhelmed and stressed. To activate mindfulness thinking at any time, just focus on the breath. When you are aware of your breathing you are in the now and mindfulness is up and running until fast thinking butts in or we choose slow thinking for a particular purpose. It works both ways. Fast and slow thinking have their place but you also don't want to persist with this mindful style of non-thinking when your house is on fire.

In adopting a mindful practise and approach to life, the challenge is whether to continue thinking in the ways we do. Yes, use the thinking mind to plan and solve problems, but also be aware that because of the nature of mind and our attachment to it, we can unconsciously wander and become caught up in the emotional content of our thoughts. The wider body and nervous system dance to the commands of the thinking mind but the body in its own way also drives the thinking mind, as when we feel pain and maybe think catastrophically that we are going to die.

The thinking mind in action is always framing things as problems to be solved. There is a sense that we can think our way out of every situation. This is not necessarily so. At times it is necessary to just be with the situation or challenge you face, beyond the emotional load that it carries, to fully know the reality of that situation. As a consequence, deeper awareness and understanding can emerge. This is the power of mindfulness. It opens us to greater possibility, choice and freedom in how we live our lives.

Nobody teaches us to be still and silent and comfortable in and with ourselves. We have to learn it from scratch. Developing the skill to be at peace with ourselves and others is profoundly important, and most enjoyable. Creating a place of peace for ourselves is the first challenge we face in this book.

2

WHAT IS MINDFUL WALKING?

We all have our own walking style. Some of us are fast walkers, who like to stride ahead with purpose. Some of us prefer to stroll, and meander along with our feet loose and arms swinging. Your walk might be more of a strut, a stride, a swagger. You might practise Nordic walking, using walking poles to help you up the mountain. Or Chi walking, a rather trendy style developed from the martial art practise of Tai Chi, involving slow, focused movement. Or do you walk with a limp? Have your legs given up on you? Do you keep your head bowed, your arms wrapped around you, and become unmindful, sometimes, forgetting to look around you?

All of these styles only begin to describe the different aspects and nuances of how we walk. I'd like to add a new style to that infinite vocabulary of movement, and that's mindful walking. In deciding to walk mindfully we deliberately incorporate the qualities of mindfulness into our daily exercise. Out walking in nature, we can gradually bring other postures of meditation, like sitting, standing or lying, into an informal mindful activity. Away from the noise and clutter of our lives we can break from our walk, stand and watch, lie down and soak up the warmth of the sun, if it comes out. Or simply sit and notice, appreciate and savour the wonder all about.

Mindful walking is about mindful movement. It is about doing, while experiencing being. While movement is crucial to us in every form, it can often be unmindful. It can just be a reaction against having to do something else that we find boring or uninteresting, when we decide to 'move on' physically and mentally. Mindful walking not only trains the mind, it trains the body. It is important to understand that mindful walking should incorporate stillness also. Sitting, lying and standing are as much a part of mindful walking as the actual walking itself.

Even on our walk we need to stop occasionally, focus and collect ourselves.

Mindful walking is a great way to move forward both physically and in a metaphorical sense, in our lives. It alerts us to the amazing adventure that is life. On the walk we focus on the process, not the outcome. It is not about chasing highs, but about noticing the exquisite beauty that is already there in front of us. There is a powerful shift in consciousness from the destination to the journey itself, from the future to the present moment.

People who find seated meditation challenging often find it encouraging to introduce some movement into their practise. Mindful walking allows for movement in even more interesting ways. Mindful walking has the effect of bringing the often overactive mind and the often underactive body into alignment. It does not have to have spiritual or religious connotations, although for some people it very much does. Mindfulness might just encompass an ability to see the wonder and awe of it all, detached from our preconceived notions of the sacred. We can connect to something greater than ourselves.

The world around us is awesome in its own right if we care to observe it mindfully.

Mindful walking also naturally brings the mind to the present. The body is always in the present. The breath is always in the present. In walking mindfully there is a very real meeting of mind, body and the wider context of our environment, beyond time. We can reconcile and integrate the vastness of all that is around us with an acceptance of our miniscule and fleeting part in it.

This is paradoxical but potentially liberating. In accepting the littleness of our place in this wider universe and the uncertainty of what we know, we can sit on a 350-million-year-old rock at the edge of a path and mindfully accept that we are part of this wonder. The endless drama of the small self fades away as we become part of that rock. Stone becomes honey in that sitting. The process of growing fully aware continues on the walk.

Focusing on the simple rhythm of the breath, the gradient of the ground, our steps and our footfall is all part of a deeper noticing. There is a lot more going on than we often realise. The heat of the sun, the breeze on our face, the sound of a passing bee, the furze at our feet, the sights, the colours, the shades of light and darkness, all coming and going. With everything changing constantly, sometimes all we can do is stand and stare in awe.

There is no such thing as a good or bad walk. We don't assess and judge the experience afterwards, as we do a batch of reps in the gym, nor do we analyse it like we do the form after a football match. The point of mindful walking is to be open without any agenda or bias about what is good or bad, a success or a disaster, and to learn from whatever we experienced. In walking mindfully, the experience might be stunning and breathtaking but we are not attached to it. We don't need to hold on to it or quickly replicate it once it's over. To walk mindfully is to experience that walk fully in the moment. If it was wondrous, accept that as a gift. If it poured raining, accept that as character-building. The next walk will be different.

Walking was always about discovery, from the first walk the earliest humans took out of Africa. And it still is. On walks throughout the world, I have always been struck by the simplicity of the exchange when you meet fellow travellers along the way. Walking is a simple activity that brings us into contact with other human beings beyond the busyness and complexity we seem to endow our lives with. It's on these walks that we rediscover the simplicity of life too. The basic, very human questions that usually emerge are: 'Where have you come from?' 'What is it like there?' 'Where are you going to?' 'Which way will you take?' There is a need to fill in the gaps and help each other on the journey. As in life, we would know very little if we were not prepared to talk and ask and share.

'As you walk, eat and travel, be where you are. Otherwise you will miss most of your life.' The Buddha

MINDFUL MOVEMENT FOR THE IMMOBILE

In the full of our health we can overlook the centrality of walking to everyday life. It is only when we are deprived of the ability to walk that we come to fully appreciate this importance. For all of us the time will eventually come when, through old age, infirmity or indeed unforeseen accident, we cannot walk as we used to. My friend Ted recently said to me, 'When I could walk, I had no mind for it and now that I can't walk very well, I would love to be able to do it.'

Some of us in our lives find that we are unable to walk in the conventional sense of bipedal locomotion, putting one foot in front of the other. What do we do then? While this book is specifically dedicated to mindful walking, it is important to understand that mindful movement is at the heart of this walking posture. We don't have to be able to walk to notice the complexity and exquisiteness of our movements. For people like Sarah, who have been unable to walk since birth, this is particularly important.

Not being able to walk does not inhibit or

prevent mindful movement and its benefits. Mindful walking, whether formal or informal, is a very special and important form of mindful movement but it is not the only form. Dance, yoga, Pilates and tai chi are all embodied forms of movement where even with an illness or disability, a mindful awareness can be brought to all the senses and the present moment of experience. Mindfulness can be brought to the practise of simple movement and stretching to loosen up. This movement is part of us from the time we first learn to crawl.

For people who through old age, physical injury or disability are unable to walk, new forms of creative movement can be mindfully explored through a simple meditation practise as described in the body scan posture in Chapter Four. You can adapt this to focus on sensations in one part of your body and incorporate gentle rhythmic movement. By repeating this every day for ten minutes, you will feel the potential for mindful movement to improve your mood and well-being.

The Dancer: Sarah's Story

Sarah is a wheelchair user who was born with spina bifida. She is a bright, intelligent and articulate woman and lives an incredibly full life. She is currently studying for a master's degree.

While she is physically restricted in that she cannot walk, this in no way prevents her mobility and movement. She drives and goes about her life and work with an energy that is impressive. For people who experience lack of mobility, her story is an inspiring account of overcoming real and perceived physical and mental limitations.

Sarah first learned about mindfulness in secondary (second level) school through the good fortune of having a substitute teacher who was a mindfulness practitioner and who shared her skill with her pupils. 'It was the first thing she did on a Thursday morning. I suppose she wanted to calm everybody down before we started,' she recalls. The meditation lasted for about 15–20 minutes and Sarah found it grounded her. From time to time, throughout her school years she also attended retreats where this practise was deepened.

I first met Sarah while teaching in a university. During the two years of the programme she not only struggled with the academic and reflective challenges of the subject like every other student, but in her second year had an unfortunate traumatic accident. The manner in which she dealt with her setback is a testament to her courage but also to the practise of mindfulness and especially mindful movement which she uniquely describes.

She is a practitioner of physically integrated dance. This creative dance form emerged out of the disability culture movement of the early 90s which set out to educate the public about disability. The disability culture movement celebrates, in a positive way, the first-person experience of disability not as a medical construct but as a real social phenomenon, where despite limitations disabled people are able to participate in activities which nourish them, mind and body.

Sarah describes how she has linked integrated

dance and movement with mindfulness. 'In dance you are in your own essence, you are in the moment, you are in your body in the movement.' In this sense Sarah is the movement, very much like how we become part of that movement when we walk mindfully.

'In integrated dance everyone is conscious at the start about who is walking and who is not. In a short time, it is about the dance and about the movement in the dance. It is not about who can't do what. Some dancers might have a bad hip or a bad back. It becomes about the movement that everyone brings to the dance.'

Mindful movement might also for Sarah be 'hopping out of my wheelchair and getting on the floor and doing some yoga.' It might be as simple as 'getting up on a recliner, mindfully stretching as I watch TV'.

Like all of us, Sarah has her moments when the thinking might tend to be negative. 'I just need to shift my mood, so it is just a case of physically moving from one place to another.' Mindful movement shifts the focus away from the negative thinking for Sarah just like mindful walking can do for others.

As part of her mindful movement practise, diarying is important to Sarah. 'It gives me a chance to see what is going on, to reflect on my experience.' This may be about something handled well or not so well. Because of Sarah's challenges, she says that she has always had an appreciation that 'life is so fleeting, it can change like that'. Like mindfulness and mindful movement, diarying keeps her grounded. 'It is a lovely gift to yourself,' she says.

Mindfulness is about mindful movement even if you are unable to walk or walk as far as you might like at this time. Perhaps you are recovering from an operation and dealing with residual pain. Mindful movement can be as simple as stretching in the bed or taking those first six steps along the hospital corridor. Of course this should always be done under medical supervision but you can notice with greater openness and curiosity how mind and body work in movement beyond any sense of limitation or disability. Whether or not you can walk, you are connected to this amazing world through movement of all sorts. You can notice and experience this movement at virtually every sensory level. Sarah practises this mindfulness of movement in a way that benefits her and enables her to live her life to the full.

WHAT MAKES MINDFUL WALKING DIFFERENT?

All walking is by definition mindful, in that it tends to interrupt the processing power of the brain. Mind and body work together in a contemplative way. It is extremely difficult to perform complex computational tasks while walking. Try it sometime. While walking at a briskish pace, subtract 17 from 373. Then do it again and again, and see how you get on. Multiply 67 by 3 and see if you might not be inclined to stop or slow down, at the very least. For most of us, to execute a mental task we need to sit down and focus our attention. For sure, thoughts and ideas will come and go as you walk and this is the wonderful side effect of it. Ancient philosophers such as Aristotle knew this contemplative side of walking. They knew how to inspire themselves. Challenges and decisions become clearer in that our whole body, at every sensory level, becomes involved in the mobile process of figuring them out. The body thinks also. 'Does it look right?' 'Does it feel right?' 'Does it smell right?' 'Does it taste right?' 'Is my heart in it?' We can find all these answers by listening to the body as we walk.

The qualities of mindfulness inform all aspects of mindful walking. This style of walking is first about slowing down, both your thoughts and your pace, to deliberately meet and greet the present moment of our unfolding experience in a focused, observant but non-judgemental way.

We mentioned earlier that in the Buddhist scriptures, mindfulness referred to mental development. When we first observe our thinking, we can notice a discomfiting reality. We're not thinking thoughts, our thoughts are thinking us. We are on autopilot. We can start to believe everything we think. Mindfulness is a kind of focused attention that allows us to see the internal workings of our mind and body. For some, this means being able to listen clearly to an ongoing internal commentary. For others, it is to see clearly the images that play like a silent movie in their heads. For many it is both.

Mindfulness is not a technique to stop this commentary or this movie. It is not about clearing our minds of interfering negative thoughts and images that we dislike. It is not some magical process that transports us to a Pollyanna place where everything is wonderful and beautiful and just as we would wish.

Many people come to mindfulness practise with the expectation that they will be able to switch off the troubling negative thoughts and the movie reel of images, as if they will be left with only positive ones. This is not the objective of mindfulness. The mind is working the way the mind works and it always will. The body knows no better and is dancing to the instructions of the mind. Simply, we'll be able to be mindful of this and accept it.

Mindfulness gives us a way of being with our mind and body experience, whether positive, negative or neutral. The attitude we choose to take helps us to settle the restless, chattering, negative and sometimes cruel wild track of thoughts and images which causes so much pain at times. As a consequence of this attitude of mindful non-judging, the body falls into line. The attitude I speak of is a calm, alert, confident way of being with the unfolding experience, whether positive, negative or neutral, and seeing the wonder of it all. In this place of mindfulness we don't believe everything we think, we just observe our thinking. By default, we can develop a means of switching off the autopilot of ingrained behaviours and habitual reactions. It's sometimes surprising, when we focus our attention on the moment at hand, what becomes visible beyond the usual mental chatter. We can maybe for the first time see more clearly this mental commentary and what may be holding us back from fully exploring our potential and experiencing our life. It is a state of alertness and calmness. These are qualities we all have but might need to reconnect with.

In developing a way to name the thoughts, emotions and sensations we live with, we can begin to tame them. In short, it helps us to notice but not judge what it is we are experiencing, positive, negative or neutral. Mindfulness is in essence an ongoing experiment in life. The principal challenge is to bring our awareness to the present moment when it includes often intense moods, feelings, emotions, thoughts, sensations, sounds, sights, smells. It is fundamentally a state of attentiveness. It is openness without any particular agenda or bias.

As we move on there will be more experiments to broaden our understanding and awareness. We will practise mindfulness in the different postures mentioned. In learning to walk mindfully, we will learn how to walk again. This is the beginning of a practise and discipline that can serve you well. In not believing everything you think about yourself, others and the world, you relax into the world and open up to a greater range of options as to how you live and relate to others. As we will see, you do not have to set out to change anything. In observing the world in a more mindful way, change looks after itself. This allows you a freedom where you are mindfully indifferent to outcomes, but positively and passionately engaged with your process of living and experiencing your life, now, this very moment.

'Do you have the patience to wait
Till your mud settles and the water is clear?
Can you remain unmoving
Till the right action arises by itself?
The master doesn't seek fulfilment.
Not seeking, not expecting,
she is present and can welcome all things.'
Lao Tzu

3

MINDFULNESS: THE PRINCIPLES AND PARADOXES

Having hopefully convinced you of the benefits of mindfulness, let us go into a little more detail about this way of being. In her book *Mindfulness-Based Cognitive Therapy*, Rebecca Crane, a research fellow within the Centre for Mindfulness Research and Practice at Bangor University in Wales, points to three broad areas of learning and practice in mindfulness:

- The development of awareness through formal mindfulness practice;

- The cultivation of an attitude and approach to our lives based on a framework of seven principles: Non-Judging, Patience, Beginner's Mind, Trust, Non-Striving, Acceptance and Letting Go;

- A mind / body understanding, and acceptance of our ultimate vulnerability. Suffering is part of our human journey. Mindfulness introduces us to ways of consciously investigating and working with the suffering and challenges we face in life.

These seven principles of mindfulness mentioned by John Kabat-Zinn in his book *Full Catastrophe Living* – Non-Judging, Patience, Beginner's Mind, Trust, Non-Striving, Acceptance and Letting Go – are in fact more than principles. They are foundational attitudes to life. These attitudes are applicable to both formal and informal mindfulness practise. There is, however, a profound paradox at the heart of mindfulness. It is the paradox of control and the suggestion that in learning not to control our thoughts and emotions, not to struggle like that fish on the hook, we have more control. That in doing nothing, in letting go, instead of relinquishing control, we gain a firmer grasp on things. This paradox of control as it applies to mindfulness is important in gaining a full understanding of the practice and its application.

THE STOCKDALE PARADOX

In his book *Good to Great*, the business consultant and lecturer Jim Collins, perhaps unwittingly, makes reference to this paradox in the context of rigid control and goal setting. For prisoners incarcerated in Hanoi during the Vietnam War, setting rigid goals to escape was a way to control but was problematic when they didn't achieve their goals. Those prisoners that had the capacity to deal with the ongoing brutal facts as they arose, with a degree of confidence in ultimate success, were more likely to be resilient and persist.

Collins tells the story of James Stockdale, a US marine pilot. On 9 September 1965, Stockdale launched his A-4 Skyhawk off the flight deck of the USS *Oriskany* on a mission over north Vietnam. Just as he was flying over his intended target his jet was hit by a missile. James Stockdale was now out of control.

Having ejected from his aircraft he parachuted and landed near a small village. A quickly assembling crowd found him and beat him mercilessly; as a consequence he further suffered a broken back, leg and a paralysed arm.

He was taken into custody as a prisoner of war and incarcerated in Hoa Lo Prison, the infamous 'Hanoi Hilton.' He was to spend the next seven years living under unimaginably sadistic and brutal conditions. He was subjected to mental and physical torture. He was kept in solitary confinement and in total darkness for four years. He was chained, starved, denied medical care and allowed no contact with others.

Drawing on his own inner resources he developed a coping strategy based on a clear understanding of how he could be most effective. He did not beat himself up for his past mistakes. He did not allow himself over-think things, such as whether, if he had banked his aircraft to the right just one degree, he might have avoided the missile hit. He did not worry too much about the future, or set goals as some of his fellow prisoners found they had to do to cope. They would set a rigid goal, such as 'I'll be out for Christmas', even when this was looking to be impossible. He knew that the only way that he could keep himself in contention and give himself the best chance of ever getting out was to focus his attention on the only moment of effective action, the now.

As Stockdale told Collins, 'You must never confuse faith that you will prevail in the end – which you can never afford to lose – with the discipline to confront the most brutal facts of your current reality, whatever they might be.' Collins calls this acceptance of the painful now while keeping faith in a brighter future 'the Stockdale paradox.'

Eckhart Tolle refers to this as *The Power of Now* in his book of the same name. While Stockdale had an education in stoic philosophy, not in Eastern meditation, the principles he applied are very much similar to mindfulness and a particular attention to and attitudinal focus on the now. In developing the practise of mindfulness, considerable power can be added to the idea of focused, conscious non-judgemental attention and observation of our thinking and emotions. The objective of this is not to control your thinking. In fact, more control is a by-product of not controlling. This is the paradox of control. You cannot change the past, you cannot predict the future, even though the egoic thinking mind will make valiant attempts to control everything for you if you let it.

In accepting vulnerability and dealing with whatever challenge he faced, Stockdale ultimately prevailed and went on to become a very successful academic and enjoyed a fulfilling personal life.

THE SEVEN PILLARS

Understanding this paradox of control is important as we now come to explore the pillars of mindfulness.

Non-Judging

The judging mind is there for a very good reason. As humans evolved, we had to constantly monitor our external environment to keep ourselves out of harm's way, and to make sure we knew who our friends were. We assumed the worst before confirming people's good intentions, by labelling and making associations and comparisons.

Twenty thousand years ago at the dangerous water hole which we shared with sabre-toothed tigers and other beasts, there was an adaptive benefit to judging things for the worse, and predicting a negative outcome. If, at the water hole, we noticed a bush rustling, it might have been the wind but it was safer to say it was a tiger lurking. If we avoided the bush and went home to the cave and in fact there was nothing behind the bush, we might have been thirsty or hungry but we were alive. The judging mind helps us to categorise and in some instances stereotype the things and people we encounter, to protect ourselves.

However, at the heart of the judging mind are unconscious drives and compulsions which can very negatively impact on our mood, feelings and emotions. This judging mind can create a prison of anxiety and depression. The judging mind can be hard and unforgiving, clogged up with opinions and attachments to notions of good or bad, right or wrong, worth or worthlessness, failure or success. This judging mind often won't allow our unfolding experience to be as it is. Rather, it will try to escape, avoid or change it in some way. This can become a pattern in our lives. In some sense, we become enslaved to this judging mind.

Your thinking, judging mind, like everyone else's, is prone to error, bias and distortion. It often gets it badly wrong, particularly when it comes to relationships. We often take our judgements to be fact. Developing the skills and strategies to distinguish judgements from facts and mindfully awarenessing – or harnessing the awareness of – our thoughts and thinking can mitigate these errors in processing, and improve our relationships and performance in many ways.

If you have managed to practise the 'Name and Tame Meditation', you might have a sense of where the ebb and flow of your thoughts is going. Where are your thoughts right now? What about sensations in the body? What is the mood of your mind right now? Is it at ease? Is it rigid and inflexible, or is it open to your potential and possibility? Can you develop a greater stillness and awareness of this mood without judging it as good, bad or indifferent?

If the present moment is the only reality we have, what is happening in it right now? Noticing is the essence of mindfulness.

We have all felt how much fun it is to be a spectator in the audience. With the right alchemy on stage we can be captivated, fully present for the show. We can focus our attention and observe the player from a distance without necessarily being involved. Of course we will tend to judge aspects of the show that determine whether we will recommend it to our friends. This is what the critics do, often with the influence to close down a Broadway show in the opening week! Mindfulness asks us to leave behind our inner critic and suspend this judging element, and search for our own truth. We are asked to be a witness to our own experience and an impartial one at that. To simply watch ourselves watching, and observe things. How did that line affect us? Where does our eye return to? Is anybody grating on our nerves? Can you begin to observe without judging or intellectualising? It is what it is. Can you be alert and calm in this process and at the same time not get lost in your thoughts of how it should be? This is hard work but it is good work. And you won't enjoy what you came to see any less.

Being judgemental is an attempt to control the exterior world. We are trying to be more certain of our surroundings and in so doing create even more anxiety and pain for ourselves. We are very hopeful creatures. We persist in doing the same things in the hope that we might get different results. But in our lack of awareness we lose sight of the possibility of change. Because we so strongly identify ourselves with our habitual negative way of doing things we become disconnected from the natural flow and changing, impermanent nature of life.

But there can be profound change with a more mindful approach. This does not arise through more thinking. It arises through seeing and understanding in a non-judging way. Steadying the mind comes from the practise of mindfulness in its many guises. As Jiddu Krishnamurti said, 'The ability to observe without evaluating is the highest form of intelligence.'

This involves moving from an ego-driven, self-centred way of viewing things to a warmer, more wide open and less personalised way of looking at our experience. Our attitude can then move to a greater acceptance of ourselves and others. It's remarkable what you can learn from just watching and waiting. As you grow and deepen your mindfulness practise, try to notice how you tend to judge and categorise your experience of life and those in it.

Patience

Mindfulness is a form of wisdom which understands that life is very uncertain and unfolds in its own time. Patience is central to mindfulness and a form of emotional intelligence we cannot do without. In all the striving to become the success we already are, we can also become impatient if we are not progressing at a pace we deem to be appropriate, or if others are not compliant in the process. On the slopes of our ambition, we become restless and impatient with life and those that undermine us. We feel entitled. We have expectations to be met. We need the validation, of course. We won't be fully confident or comfortable with ourselves until we get validation from others. We may need so much of it there won't be enough room on our headstone. We are swamped by the imaginary things we would like people to think about us. All of this comes at a cost and life doesn't unfold according to any plan. We may become ill. Our husbands or partners or children may become ill. We may lose our job. What then? We need our resources more than ever in these undermining times.

Impatience sits well with the judging mind. What drives this impatience is perhaps a sense that we have not got enough done and we need to be somewhere else to do it. We can tend to see others as a hindrance, to be climbed over or pushed to one side in our rush to get elsewhere.

Underlying impatience can settle into frustration, and a sense that we cannot change things in our lives. We are dissatisfied with what we find. Arising from this perception and assessment that things are unalterable, we can uncover resentment. Resentment is a form of 'already listening', as the coach and author Alan Sieler describes it. This means that we are in a negative, resentful mind state where the slightest perceived offence can launch us into a full-blown 'emotional hijack.' This is a private and toxic conversation with the self. In this mind state, some of us can move very quickly to playing the victim. Anger, on the other hand, is a very public conversation. We can be literally out of our minds and out of control. We refuse to accept the way things are. Blame can follow apace. Of course, in the very short term anger can empower a persecutor, but only if they find a compliant victim and it is not without its consequences.

In practising mindfulness we are open to a more patient approach to the natural unfolding of our experience. We don't approach life aggressively or avoid it timidly. We know when to give ourselves a rest and when to assert ourselves in an emotionally intelligent, adult manner. Even when things are going against us, we don't let our attachment to certain outcomes or results dominate our thinking in this moment. Setting some time aside to be with our thoughts and notice our emotions, we can cultivate a mindful approach and accept whatever conditions there are, favourable or not so. We always have the choice to accept.

Beginner's Mind

Too often we can get stuck in the confining rut

of our own learned and inherited thinking, our own emotional and behavioural styles. We fancy we have seen it all before. We know it all. This is not the case if we care to stand and stare. There is extraordinary in the very ordinary. How are we to open our eyes to wonder from an early age? The education most of us get does us some disservice, in teaching us by rote and expecting us to have the knowledge to produce the right answer. The creativity and freedom of childhood exploration and learning is sometimes snuffed out.

Far too often, we let the knowledge we have accumulated drown out our potential to be lifelong, open and curious learners. Such an approach also blinds us to things as they are, right in front of us. We miss much of the colour and richness of the present moment. A new bridge has been built in the city, but we are on a work phone call as we cross it, so we don't question the marvel of its construction. We don't see the buds appearing next to the tree trunk, because winter has made us stern, our sense implacable. Not knowing, wrapped up in an attitude of curiosity and an openness to learn, even from mistakes, is a powerful recipe for well-being and happiness.

Beginner's Mind is a wonderful departure point from which to explore our experience, to observe how we construct it. We might even increase our awareness of the continually changing nature of that experience. It might help us to bring clarity to how we perceive things around us. In adopting a more curious approach, we might even get to a place where we are comfortable with asking the question 'How sure am I with what I do know? What else do I need to know?'

You might like to take some time to reflect on what all this means to you now. Perhaps turn to your diary and write it all out. Can this step help you to deal with the mindless fear of not knowing and bring you into the present moment, where you can be an open learner to maybe know more? It is ok that we just don't know. It is just fine to be uncertain about a lot of things, especially things in the future. In the certain mind there are few possibilities; in Beginner's Mind there are many. Which is your choice?

Trust

As we have seen, we have very creative ways

of protecting and defending ourselves against uncertainty. Notwithstanding, trust is a core value that goes to the heart of human functioning at both individual and group levels. To trust is to have confidence in the wide unknown. Developing trust in ourselves and our thinking, emotions and the sensations in our bodies is a powerful part of mindfulness and its practise. In developing this practise we are making a clear statement that we are willing to take responsibility for self in every aspect we are able to.

Because of the knowledge-driven methodologies in which many of us are educated, there can be a tendency to look elsewhere than within for guidance when we struggle to provide the right answer. 'The teacher will have the right answer,' we are taught to believe. We are disciplined by a system wherein, if the answer isn't right, then you have failed. This approach doesn't favour trial and error learning wherein we build confidence in learning from mistakes and error.

If we don't trust ourselves, we settle into the comfortable assumption that others have a better answer. For sure, others have a different, often richer experience and learning to us. They can share that learning and experience with us but they cannot live our life for us.

We live in a world of so-called 'experts' – whether economists, medical professionals, lawyers, beauty therapists. Yes, people have richer experience and they may be perceived to be experts in their field, but life and work is moving so fast that it is hard to keep up. Many people feel disillusioned when the experts are seen to be fallible – to have given the wrong advice, overcharged us, sold us something we didn't want. In dealing with the complex problems we all face, we need ourselves to take responsibility and to trust our own judgement and contribution.

With the proliferation of experts in life, there is an ever greater need for us to trust our own feelings and follow our intuition on what is the right thing to do. In developing the confidence to observe and be with our unfolding experience we are taking responsibility. We are accountable for our actions and, eventually, for our mind state. Trusting ourselves empowers us. It builds a belief that our own experience is as valid as that of the next person's. The more we bring the ego under our control the more we will begin to trust ourselves and by, extension, others.

The underlying reason for practising mindfulness is to unlock our own potential. To do that, our intuition must be brought into play. Therein lies our potential, which is an untapped wisdom we can all find the source to. Wisdom is in us all, though it might be hidden. The challenge is to unlock that wisdom and trust in who we are.

Developing trust in yourself can also mean that you are more comfortable with your limitations, your vulnerability. Trust in yourself allows you to be at ease and more compassionate with yourself and others. Developing trust within groups allows people to come out and be their authentic selves, and make their unique contribution. Good leaders create that trust but sometimes, we have to instigate it ourselves in our small, unseen way.

Non-Striving

There is very little in our lived experience that doesn't have a purpose. For the most part, we are driven to get somewhere or achieve something. Striving and achievement were in the human DNA in order for us to survive the jungle, to find nourishment and create shelter and kinship. In the 21st century our goals are more elaborate and interconnected globally, and life is made easier for us. And yet we still have the same tendency to strive. We build. We improve. We devour knowledge. We seek for fun. How often do we just be, as human beings? We perhaps could more correctly be called human doings. The modern environment overloads us with choice, information and distractions that can become terribly exhausting. The most pressing need is to create some space to slow down and reconnect. Mindfulness meditation is about just being in that space.

The mantra of the busy, 'doing' mind is 'Don't just sit there, do something.' The mantra of the non-striving, 'being' mind is 'Don't just do something, sit there.' Or stand, or lie there for a little while. In mindfulness, all the goal theory is binned. Your goal doesn't even need to be 'Be more mindful.' You can just be, mindfully. Like now. Finding your breath again, feeling its rhythms.

Taking note of the situation you are sitting in as you thumb this book, and recognising how it makes you feel. Accepting that feeling. There is no goal other than being here as you are now. You are invited just to be yourself, here and now. You *are* yourself, here and now, already.

For the newcomer to mindfulness this can be a very challenging, even disturbing idea to fathom. There can be a sense that you should be getting more out of this meditation. You should be feeling considerably less stressed. It should be better. This is the very struggle and the style of thinking of the judging mind that got you here in the first place, so something different is needed. The other principles begin to fit when you consider patience, curiosity and trust as the bedrocks of simply being. You are the observer. Thoughts, feelings, sensations come and go. That is it. You are where you are. No need to be anywhere else. The now is the only moment you ever have. It is as it is.

This whole process actually makes some sense when we fully accept that the past is gone and the future will look after itself. The now is the only moment of insight and knowing. In a paradoxical way, to focus on this moment is to keep us in contention for a better future, beyond mindless doing and worrying about what may never happen. We achieve our goals not by striving but by non-striving.

Acceptance

At the heart of mindfulness is a greater openness and receptiveness. Once filled with new possibilities, we feel a freshness that allows us to focus on what is actually happening in our mind and body. This is about seeing the ego in intimate detail. We ordinarily avoid, reject and deny unpleasant experiences. Understandably, we tend to approach attractive, delicious things like chocolate and wine and want to consume them in quantities. We attach ourselves to pleasant experiences. We can also slip into boredom when our experience is neutral.

In many ways we deny or resist the negative issues we face. This is so very natural when we face catastrophic setbacks like bereavement. We deny. We are angry. We ask, why me?

We struggle with terrible news and can get sucked in to the pain and suffering. We never want to be in that place of pain, so we do what we can to move away from it. We expend a lot of energy in the process. We describe what we love. We justify our approach. We might dispense blame on others. We hold on, and the pain and struggle goes on. We want to go backwards, to the times we were content and safe. We can't seem to go forwards. In holding ourselves back we deny our potential, our wisdom, we reject our true selves. It can add additional layers to the pain and suffering that is already there. This is all part of losses such as bereavement. Through developing a mindful practise, the pain and loss will diminish and new possibilities may emerge in time. We may have to go through periods of anger and denial in the process of acceptance.

There are still challenges and setbacks to be encountered on the journey. Mindfulness cannot remove these. Pain, suffering and grief are part of the arc of life but mindfulness can make these challenges more manageable.

Grief doesn't always mean losing somebody. There is grief in the overwhelming disappointment we feel when we haven't achieved our dreams. 'Good grief!' people used to exclaim, when something wasn't going to plan. We experience loss on a much lesser scale when we don't get what we wish for: a house we pictured living in, a respect we'd dreamt of earning in our role at work, or a family we never got around to being part of. We may have to go through a lower-grade grieving process to come to terms with these losses. Accepting, in the mindful sense, does not mean that we have to like everything we experience or be passive to it. It does not mean abandoning our principles and values. It just means that we always have the choice to slow down, to observe things as they really are in this moment. However bad it is, we can be with it in the knowledge that the intensity will diminish and, in a paradoxical way, this acceptance that the situation is as it is gives us more choices and room to manoeuvre.

In resisting or rejecting whatever it is we experience, positive, negative or neutral, we continue the gloomy and self-denying patterns we've accidentally set ourselves, with no possibility to change either the viewing or the doing. Mindful acceptance creates an invisible space in our unfolding experience where we can heal. This space allows time for appropriate responses, for not perpetuating the emotional reactions which keep us stuck. In time, it can allow us to move on with our lives as best we can.

Letting Go

In our very human efforts to make our lives more bearable we cling to safe structures: routines and practises, beliefs and ideas. Time passes, and we are still clinging to these structures. We attach ourselves to the familiar in the hope that it will remain constant and make us happy. In many ways this clinging holds us back from the amazing possibility of our adventuresome, moment-to-moment experience.

Mindful observation of these thoughts and ideas presents the different possibility of non-attachment. This is not in the sense of putting our safe structures out of our head or pushing them away. It is in the sense of attuning to them and letting the experience be as it is, moment by moment. In adopting such a stance, the ideas and attachments can lose their power because they are known for what they are. They are only constructs, albeit persistent and resistant constructs of the mind.

When the penny drops and we become aware of our absorption and attachments, to ideas, judgements and opinions, it is as if a whole new world of wonder and possibility opens up. Wonder is a childlike way to look at the world, a continual fascination with things, events and circumstances we may not have experienced before. Rather than escaping the new and unfamiliar, it is about a willingness to live in the moment. The letting go can be a release, sometimes a painful release, from a lifetime of conditioned and habituated thinking, emotions and behaviours, which for the most part are unconscious and outside of awareness. It can be heart-rending to have to relinquish what we know.

To reduce the stress and the strains of life, to be peaceful and happy, we can always choose to accept the things we don't like when they appear at our doorstep. We also have the choice to let go of the things we welcome and wish to cling on to. The source of most of our suffering is in our minds. Both positive and negative visitors to our minds are equal imposters to be treated with respect, equanimity and balance. In shining the light of mindfulness in a compassionate and non-judgemental way on our lives from time to time, there are no shadows from the past beyond learning, and no imaginings for the future beyond the unfolding reality of the present moment.

Mindfulness practise can take us beyond our fearful, anxious, defensive, insecure and clutching ego and onto the path of our potential and wisdom. In mindfulness, our potential is much greater than our ego. We may in time discover that if we had no self to worry about, we would have no problems.

Non-Judging, Patience, Beginner's Mind, Trust, Non-Striving, Acceptance and Letting Go are quite powerful points of reference to return to. We now bring those seven foundational attitudes to our mindfulness practise. Now and again, try to return to these bedrocks and reflect on their meaning to you. Developing any practise involves commitment and discipline.

4

MINDFULNESS: THE FORMAL PRACTISE

While mindfulness practise is the key to mindful walking, it is also the hardest aspect. While the thinking, conceptual mind can maybe see the logic and the rationale of mindfulness, the practise is a great challenge to that thinking mind. There is always something else to do. A friend of mine tells me regularly that she is much too busy for this mindfulness thing. It takes a commitment and discipline to set aside the time to learn and practise the necessary skills, but anyone can do this.

As we alluded to previously, this could be the beginning of a new way of life. The skills of breathing, sensing, feeling, eating, smelling, walking and every other human activity beyond sleeping are there already but they can be enriched in a more mindful and beneficial way.

This chapter covers some introductory aspects to the practise of mindfulness but I also strongly recommend trying out a formal programme of mindfulness, using an app or CD, or joining a local group. After this we will move on to explore mindful walking in action, where you can incorporate your mindfulness practise into a life-giving physical movement that bonds both body and mind.

IN THE BEGINNING

Let's consider the core aspects of mindfulness as you set out on this new adventure, this new form of learning. You are now actually dipping your toe in the waters of your mind, be they stormy or calm. The formal meditation postures of sitting, lying, standing and walking will be introduced before we go on to consider mindful walking as an informal practise in its own right, applicable in every aspect of your life. To begin with, this book asks you to commit to 10 minutes every day.

Where?

Mindfulness is about reconditioning your mind. But to do this we must see the link between mind and body, so if possible, first take some time to create a peaceful and calm environment, free from distractions. Learning to concentrate mindfully is difficult in its own right so reducing any additional external cause for interference is quite vital in the early stages. Find a safe, quiet, uncluttered and as pleasant as possible place to sit. Depending on the season and its elements, this can be indoors or out of doors. It might be on a chair at the kitchen table or by a window in the living room. You could light a candle, and place a cushion at your back. Create your own bespoke special but simple place, as it were.

When?

Deciding when to fit in your practise takes some careful thought. Selecting a time when you are not too tired and when there is little or no activity around you gives the best chance to ease your way into the practise without losing concentration. You may have to experiment with what works best for you. I suggest you try different times for a few days, as you want to be relaxed yet sufficiently alert.

Play to your strengths. Because I am a morning lark, getting up a little earlier in the morning to create the time and space works very well for me. Before your day starts in earnest, you are often at your most calm and at a time when you are least likely to be interrupted in your practise. If you're a night owl, who only comes alive after dark, later in the day is likely to bring you better dividends.

How long?

Initially we are asking you to set aside 10 minutes per day, for each of the four postures described below. As you progress and strengthen your practise, you could extend this to 20 or even 40 minutes. Use a timer or one of the apps on your smartphone to time your meditation. Some of the apps have nice meditation bells to help you focus and remind you when the time is up. Whatever period of time you do devote, make a daily effort to practise because the benefits are gradual over time. Even if you can only commit to five minutes daily, deliver on that.

POSTURES

Sitting Meditation

At this stage we don't wish to complicate matters. While you can cultivate mindfulness skills in any position, sitting is the classic one. It is a matter of reversing your 'doing' to just 'being.' While the more advanced positions like the lotus – sitting cross-legged, with feet resting on opposite thighs – work very well, you might prefer to develop these over time; at the beginning just sitting on a chair is quite ok. You can do a few things to make sitting meditation easier. Sit upright without using the back of the chair for support. Keep your feet flat on the floor without crossing them. Keep your back straight but not rigid. Let your upper body soften into a dignified posture. This position promotes alertness and calmness and assists you in remaining still. Find a comfortable place for your hands, on your knees or on your lap. You can either keep your eyes open or closed.

To begin the actual practise of mindful meditation it helps to have an anchor for the mind. This can be found in a number of ways depending on the tradition, like using a mantra or focusing on an object. For the purpose of introducing you to meditation, the breath is the anchor to which we will always return.

Mindfulness is explained at its most basic as a focus on in-breath and out-breath, inhalation and exhalation. Your breathing is happening all the time and is influenced by your state of mind. Your breathing never happens in the past or the future. It is now. Just think, your breaths arrive in twos except for the first one and the last one. Your breath is always with you and you can return to it at any time once you choose to focus. Focusing on your breathing calms the busy mind. It also provides an opportunity to observe that mind.

Your mind wanders. Bring it back to the breath. It wanders again. Bring it back again. Focusing on your breathing is an exercise in awarenessing your mind and its wanderings. Perhaps now you can see the connection between the thinking mind and the non-thinking mind where, in awareness, you have the insight and the choice 'whether or not to think' (to reiterate a phrase from earlier). Where is your mind now? What kinds of thoughts are going on? What memories are coming up? What plans are being made?

In this exercise you just sit and watch your breathing. It sounds so simple. What's the problem? The problem always is your wandering mind because the mind has not been trained to focus on the breathing. In developing a greater awareness of the breathing you are developing the power of the 'experiencing self' Daniel Kahneman refers to – the self that experiences life based on the reality of this moment, positive, negative or neutral. Developing your mental and emotional capacity to come back to this moment of the breath is a powerful strategy for well-being, happiness and peace. It promotes calmness and a focused attention which gives you a bounty of things to consider beyond the narrow focus of 'me.' In focusing on your inner being and observing the inner movie of your mind, the walls of fear and failure can seem ill-constructed and very fragile. You can break free from them. Here and now, under the light of a focused calmness, our worries and anxieties can appear illusory. In observing the false messages of the ego, you can begin to make new meaning for yourself.

If focusing on the breath is the first part of reconditioning the mind, then scanning the body is the second part of introductory formal practise.

Lying Meditation and a Body Scan

The body scan uses some of the same skills of focused concentration as the sitting, breathing meditation. Some teachers introduce the body scan to new practitioners first. I tend to work with the sitting meditation first. But when you have the space to lie comfortably, this is a very worthwhile exercise.

This meditation directs your focused attention on the extended nervous system of the body. It is a practise of systematically surveying the body. You learn to read the body and its associated sensations and you tune into these. It can be practised in either a sitting or a lying position. Whether sitting or lying it is always good to wear warm, comfortable clothes and maybe use a cushion and yoga mat if you are lying on the floor.

When you are ready, lie down on your back, face up with hands open and palms up. Allow your body to relax and settle into the surface. Align your legs, and let your feet fall open in a V shape. Focus your attention on your breathing and try to notice the sensations the breath brings, maybe even the coldness of the air at your nostrils. Be aware of the natural flow of your breathing and the rise and fall of the tummy and lower abdomen.

Your mind, as it does, will inevitably wander away. As with the sitting meditation, gently return your attention to the in-breath and the out-breath. In this way you give yourself the best chance of being calm and relaxed and fully present to your moment-to-moment experience in the now.

Now bring your attention down to your feet. Be aware of any sensations of hot or cold, strain or soreness. Moving up your legs, pay attention to your calves and shins, and as your mind wanders, worries and reaches into the future, try to bring it back to your breath. Your mind will wander. It is what it is. As you breathe out, let go of any tension.

Move further up to your thighs and buttocks, adopting the same openness and curiosity to the sensations you discover. Let your legs relax.

Bring your attention to the core of your body, and in turn to your back, chest and abdomen where we can hold a lot of our tension. Be aware of the breath. Breathe in and out. Relax into the surface you are lying on.

Bring your attention now to your neck and shoulders. Again this is an area in the body where tension may be held. Let the tension dissolve, as it were.

Now focus on the head, the crown, forehead, top of the head. In all the parts of the body scanned you may feel tightness, pressure, stiffness, tingling sensations. There may be the inclination to itch. There may be the wish to get up and leave. Be open to it all. Just observe it and know it in a new way.

Observe your body in its entirety. It is one amazing system, responding to and processing all the necessary working elements in tandem with the brain to maintain your overall effective functioning on the journey of this meditation, as you sit there or lie there.

Over time this practise can take as long as you wish. It may be as detailed as you wish. You might decide just to focus on your left hand throughout the scan. You could focus on the wrist, all the fingers, the fingertips, the nails and so on. Your curiosity is endless, much like your unfolding experience. The challenge is to bring it into focus.

Both the seated and body scan meditations give you the opportunity to practise this seemingly simple but quite challenging process.

Standing Meditation

The essence of mindfulness in whatever posture

you choose is dignity. Some use the image of the mountain to describe this, standing silently as the winds and clouds and rain swirl around and about. If we are to maintain hope and confidence and build resilience, we must take this stance sometimes against the chaos of life. It is always in the knowledge that the weather will change and the sun will shine.

As you stand now with feet slightly apart, back straight, head upright, allow your eyes to close. Bring awareness to your whole body and notice any physical sensations. The feet in contact with the ground. A slight sense of the body being in motion. Even in the standing posture, you can scan the body and check in with it. Even while standing you can always come back to the breath.

As you stand on the soles of your feet be open to the experience, as if you were standing for the first time. What thoughts are arriving at you, like waves curling into the beach? What intensity do they bring with them? Are they uncomfortable in any way? Do they bring excitement? Can you notice without judging whether these thoughts are positive, negative or indifferent?

If you do feel some tension or discomfort in the body, bring your attention to the specific area, concentrate your breath on that area and then let it go. You might repeat to yourself, 'It is what it is.' How does that part of the body feel now? This is an experiment in noticing what the complexity of sensations in your body at a given moment amount to. Each sensation might continue, but over time, as you know, it all passes. Our attempts to push the messages from our body away or hold on to them for too long are ultimately doomed to failure, and only prolong an unnecessary struggle.

While we stand, the qualities of mindfulness make sense. In standing mindfully we cultivate the qualities mentioned previously, such as curiosity and an openness to all experience. We are released from the hook of our own impatience, attachment and struggling.

And we prepare to collect our breath, relax our leg muscles and walk mindfully.

Walking Meditation and a Mindful Walk

The aim of formal mindful walking, like other forms of mindfulness, is to develop a deeper awareness of your experience in this instance of moving. It is to train the mind to pay close attention to the process of walking, one step at a time. Two quite wonderful things can arise in walking mindfully. You are unlikely to become either drowsy or restless, as can happen in mindful sitting – instead you become energised. And, slowing down to walk mindfully promotes a calmness and alertness. The walk provides for slow, deliberate movement which is an antidote to restlessness.

As in all new mindfulness practises it is important to give yourself a good start and reduce the possibility for distraction and interruption. Begin by finding a location that suits your purpose.

While there are many settings in which to develop your mindful walking practise, the setting does not need to be impressive for now. It can be as compact as the hallway in your home and eventually, as large and expansive as the slopes of the Andes. There are many paths and levels in between as we will see.

To start, set out a distance of five to twenty paces from start to finish. The challenge is to maintain the focus of your awareness on each step and if your mind wanders away, bring your attention back with gentleness and compassion to each of those steps. Time and again, bring your attention back.

As in the sitting meditation there is no best time for practising. It is up to you. If you've recently had a meal and are putting time aside to meditate, gentle walking helps avoid drowsiness and aids digestion. To start, come to attention by standing at your tallest with a straight back, shoulders relaxed and feet slightly apart. Let your hands hang by your sides and take some slow, deep breaths to restore your whole body for movement.

For a mindful walk, we ask you to begin as slowly as you can, as if these were your first steps. It might feel silly taking slow, exaggerated steps, but then, the first people who practised modern Tai Chi might have felt silly, and that slow martial art now has clubs in towns all over the world. Hopefully soon, everyone will begin stepping slowly and walking mindfully.

While in the standing position, scan your body from the soles of your feet to the top of your head. Observe the sensations in your body, noticing any tensions that emerge. Notice also any other sense you get of your wider surroundings regarding smell or sound, especially if you are out of doors. Return to the breath if your mind begins to wander.

Now beginning with the right foot, take one step forward at a slow, even and relaxed pace. Notice the curve of the foot as you plant it before moving forward with the left foot. Bring your attention to your breath, down through to your legs. Inhale, exhale, with each step. You can create your own rhythm. Notice how powerful your legs are, as they support you. Continue walking in this slow and mindful way until you reach the end of your designated path; it might only be four steps. Pause momentarily to notice where the mind is. You can then turn around and repeat the process.

Over time you can vary your practise. You

may wish to pause after each step to emphasise present-moment awareness. At each pause and before you proceed with the next step, you might like to imagine letting go of some anxiety or attachment, and moving on to the next moment without it. You might wish to appreciate and savour some aspect of your moment-to-moment experience, like the sweet sound of a bird singing.

If you are indoors or out in a safe and suitable location you could walk in your socks, or barefoot. Notice any sensations in your feet as they encounter the ground. Enjoy each step as it synchronises with your breath. As Thich Nhat Hanh says, allow your feet to kiss the earth you walk on. Keeping your eyes open throughout, bring the focus of your attention to a point of about five or six feet in front of you. Indoors, it could be the corner of a picture frame. Outdoors, it could be a chimney top or a tree branch. As the point grows larger, you can visualise the progress of your steps.

Skill in mindful walking only comes with intention. To be true to your intention, you need commitment, and to create a consistent practise you can fit it in with your other needs, like heading to work, going to the shop, walking up flights of stairs. Setting aside some time for concentrated practise also builds the muscle of mindfulness over time. This formal mindful walking becomes a rich journey, in which you gain awareness of the moments in your life. Sometimes we sleepwalk, without awareness of those moments. With mindful walking you can engage with your unfolding experience, one step at a time. This basic mindful walking practise can now be taken to some of the informal settings which we will shortly go on to describe.

THE WELL OF SILENCE

Guided meditations are very worthwhile. But because of the crowded nature of the mind and our unfamiliarity with silence these days, it is also useful to begin to experience silence. Once we get comfortable with silence, its simple power can do an enormous amount of the heavy lifting in our life.

For people with busy minds full of chatter

and commentary, silence can be difficult. If you take time to listen to people, it can seem like an ongoing external commentary on everything. The internal commentary never seems to stop either. Developing comfort with silence, seeing it as a friend, we don't need to talk as much.

Through mindfulness, silence can penetrate our mind and body in a way that isn't threatening. It can release the inner wisdom and potential that is within but we have to be prepared to listen first.

It is only in silence that we can really become self-aware. Only when we switch off the chorus of the world can we listen to the voices inside, the expressions of our thoughts and feelings and emotions. It is only in silence that we can become aware of our style, our way of explaining the world. It is only in silence that we can really reflect on our experience and make new meaning for ourselves. Silence, if we let it, facilitates change.

Mindfulness practise creates some silence in our day, to let it work its power. Silence allows us to develop an intimacy with our own mind and body experience that is liberating.

Freedom allows us to be mindfully indifferent to outcomes, but positively and passionately engaged with the process of living and experiencing our life, now, this very moment. In this place, our thoughts are not thinking for us, our emotions are not defining us. They are there of course, but we don't become attached or hooked. We don't take the bait. We are just who we are, whole, authentic and at peace with ourselves and the world.

Moment by moment, let today be our teacher and inspire us patiently and non-judgementally to accept and let go. On the journey, welcome every experience, whether it's positive, negative or leaves us cold. What is it trying to teach us?

It's interesting to note that *inspirare* in Latin means to breathe.

A GREAT STRUGGLE

We normally struggle with things we perceive to be uncomfortable or unfair. We feel entitled not to have these things happen to us. We wake at night and we fret about getting back to sleep.

We don't like a person and we easily bristle in their company, take offence at them. We don't like a situation and we think moving away will resolve the issue. What would it take to approach the vicissitudes of life in curiosity and wonder, without expectation of ourselves, others, or of what life presents? What could we learn when freed of the need to prove ourselves right or wrong?

Nobody said this mindfulness in all its forms and postures would be easy but it is different to the manner in which you may be currently engaging with some aspects of your experience. Life is an experiment. Devoting time to mindfulness practise can change your habits of mind and those conditioned behaviours that may not be serving you well. You have choice, you can always experiment. You can always change.

Breaking the Silence: Tim's Story

Tim is an intelligent, witty, articulate and sensitive person with a painful past and an amazing future. Having met Tim through my mindful walk and talk coaching programme, he agreed to share with us important elements of his learning and integration of mindfulness. Tim walked the metaphorical mountain of his panic attacks regularly for 12 years before I met him. When we met he talked a lot. He was restless. He described with great intelligence and in some detail how these attacks were preventing him from enjoying his life to the full. It wasn't that he was unable to function. He held down a good job, as a sales representative for a multinational company. His balanced exterior life didn't change the fact that on occasions, he found himself in the grip of fear.

On one such occasion he was in Amsterdam. 'I went on a Friday and returned on the Sunday,' Tim recalls. 'In those two nights and three days I did leave the hotel even though I really didn't want to. It was a horrible experience; I was truly terrified at times. I was having thoughts of choking and dying or vomiting in my sleep and dying. I lay awake in pure fear. At one point my body was involuntarily shaking!'

Over the 12 years he went to therapy and counselling on and off. He persevered in search of an answer. Over a period of time coaching Tim and interpreting his style, it was apparent that his threat detection system and fight / flight response could go to full-on red alert, quickly and catastrophically in times of stress. The manner in which he was interpreting the sensations of fear in his body had painful consequences for how he lived his life.

The sequence of events in a panic attack is as follows. There is always an internal (thought) trigger or external trigger which leads to a sense of unease and apprehension in the body, such as tightness in the chest, palpitations or nausea. When the body is under this amount of pressure, thoughts can go into 'flight' mode and catastrophise what's happening. The sensation in the body is not mindfully interpreted as just a sensation that will inevitably pass, but rather catastrophically, that something awful is going to happen. This is a cycle which feeds further bodily sensations and further catastrophisation. This cycle kept Tim in a grip of fear. The power of the mind to interpret a perceived threat through our senses is phenomenal. In Tim's case the brain and body are working in tandem in very undermining ways. Panic attacks are often a by-product of anxiety, which most people experience at some point in life. While our responses to perceived threat may not be as painful as Tim's, we are all prone to negative thinking and we can take offence, negatively reacting to people and events to protect our sense of self, our ego.

Our flow of conscious experience very much arises from our thoughts, perceptions, interpretations, emotions and actions. The link between our thinking, emotions, moods, feelings and behaviours is a crucial one. Our body does not know the difference between a thought in our head and a real and present danger to our physical self. Negative thoughts in our head, or as Tim describes it, 'the negative movie in my head', stimulate the same negative fight or flight reaction as a real threat from a dangerous animal our ancient predecessors would have experienced. The challenge for Tim was to devise a strategy to break the link between the thought and the fear reaction in his body.

Mindfulness can provide the space for insight and awareness but in Tim's case, a silent mindful practise was unlikely to calm the restless, hyperactive mind/body process and break the connection. Mindfulness, for all its benefits, may not serve people undergoing this type of stress. Tim did not need to go back to the movie in his head. It was time to move but move mindfully.

Over a period of time 'walking and talking' around his local city with his coach, the connection between mind and body was made. With movement, Tim was slowly able to observe the hypersensitive trigger of his emotions. Time was taken to stand and stare. Time was taken to sit and notice. This was a confidence-building process of taking on little challenges with a view to building to an ultimate one. Eventually, he decided (agreed) to get out of the city and spend a full day walking and climb a not insignificant hill in the process.

'I could have even chosen not to turn up,' Tim says. He recalls how the irrational, illogical and negative thinking kicked in at the beginning of the tranquil walk. 'My walking companion could abandon me on the mountain and throw away the car keys,' he thought. 'I'm going to walk for half an hour and be exhausted.' 'How long is it going to be?' He recalls: 'Yes, but then I decided to go on and that was it. I do remember I was constantly talking and rambling on and asking questions.'

After some time, I suggested to Tim that we walk on in silence for a while. It was obvious from Tim's body language that this was perhaps the last thing he needed. Tim later confirmed this. '"Walk in silence for a while," you said. Silence, I don't need silence, I thought, I need answers. I'll go back to the car. I'm not feeling well.' Habituated and conditioned negative ways of thinking and behaving can be hard to change, but he persisted. He took one more step.

Then a new scenario arose in Tim's head.

'What if it clouds in and we get lost?' He'd catch himself running with the scenario and try to dispute it. 'Sure, the helicopter would come then and I wouldn't have to walk down the mountain. Anyway, he knows what he is doing.'

As we moved on and began to gain height, something was beginning to change in Tim's body language. It seemed to be a bit looser, yet more upright. His head was lifting. He was stopping occasionally and looking around as the panorama unfolded.

'Inevitably you start feeling your legs and feet, feeling your back. I was paying attention to what I was doing because I was moving. The body is always here and now.'

We walked on. The movie was still running in Tim's head. He asked himself, 'After two hours in silence, why am I doing this? It makes no sense. But then maybe it will make stuff better for me in a couple of weeks – day-to-day stuff less painful.'

Silence was broken as we sat and ate lunch. We ate mindfully. Food never tastes as good as when you are high on the mountain, because of the altitude, but this gives a special flavour to mindfulness. There is a natural mindfulness that comes from slowing down and fully engaging with your surroundings and the amazing panorama. We sat for nearly an hour. We walked on to the end of the walk and parted company.

Throughout the day there were glimpses of mindfulness to be caught, walking, standing or sitting. For Tim, it was only later that pennies began to drop.

'It was a challenge. You could only get to this place on foot. It was remote.'

'Achievement – it's something to be proud of. It was high enough. It wasn't just like walking around the estate on the flat. There was a satisfaction afterwards. I had accomplished something that I didn't think I could do hours beforehand. I had broken a kind of barrier.'

'It was the satisfaction for me of realising, I'm actually helping myself, doing something for myself.' Taking action and taking responsibility for oneself is at the heart of mindful walking. If, for example, you are sitting in a comfortable chair and decide to take one step from it, you are taking action and moving from your comfort zone, as it were. You can always build on simple beginnings. In Tim's case, over time, he had grown the challenge for himself. He was now moving forward, step by step, on the mountain. He says, 'It felt like I was actually doing something to improve my situation.' Anyone can improve their situation. However, taking responsibility and taking action are the starting points. 'On the mountain we could see so far. The scope of it! So much else going on outside of what is in your head. I was also more attuned, more connected, to certain sounds that were a lot more subtle than you would find in the city.'

'I guess you have to pay more attention to the sounds when you are there on the mountain than you would in other places because you take it for granted what a car sounds like, what people passing by sound like. I remember being a lot more present than I would have been previously when I was on autopilot, arguing with myself.'

'I love having that "I did something yesterday" feeling.'

'I do remember when you said that we were going to walk in silence. It was like, how is silence going to help? Nothing happens when you are silent. I just thought I wasn't getting the information I needed to solve my problem. After a while it made sense, that the problem I had wasn't external. It was internal and the only way to hear the internal was silence.'

'It was the internal dialogue. I hadn't noticed before that there was an internal dialogue.'

That day on the mountain there was no magic, no miracles, just hard, patient work. It gave an opportunity for Tim to reconnect with his mind and body and the real world beyond the interfering noise of his mind. Over the following weeks, Tim's long walk to freedom from panic continued.

'That night I woke at 4am. For some reason I had a nightmare about bungee jumping, falling off a height. I woke up and had a full-blown 10/10 panic attack. This time I didn't resist it. I didn't distract myself from it or avoid it. I just lay there in silence. I said to myself, don't resist it.'

'The next day I was shook. I was completely and utterly exhausted. I couldn't sit still. And then at 11am, alone in my house, I curled up in a ball on the couch and started bawling, bawling. Absolute wailing, couldn't stop, didn't want to stop. It did stop.'

'Later that evening I told my partner. I remember saying to her, "I think it is leaving, the anxiety is leaving. I think I am breaking through." That was letting go. That was not resisting. I realised it is ok to cry, even for 40 minutes. Nothing bad is going to happen. Don't resist the fact that you are suffering. Don't resist the pain. It's just that you are suffering now.'

'So, even now, when I have tinges of anxiety, feelings of heat in my chest, I know that the body just still hasn't caught up with the rest. It certainly has caught up a whole lot more than it did six, seven or eight months ago.'

For Tim, the mountain provided an opportunity to walk and talk and slow down mindfully and engage mind and body. It also provided an opportunity to, paradoxically, and more importantly, walk and not talk; or over a mindful lunch, talk and not walk. We got comfortable in silence, and let it do the heavy lifting. In the busy world of incessant doing, Tim had no time to really listen to himself and observe and temper the conditioned, habituated patterns that were wearing down his morale. Mindful walking on the mountain provided a context for Tim to begin the process of realigning mind, body and spirit.

But he had to take that first step and begin the patient process of accepting and letting go. In taking a less judging stance he now trusts himself in a deeper way. In walking mindfully we can always change the way we relate to our experience. Tim was waking up.

This story always makes me go back to thinking about heart, mind and body. Like all of us, Tim, deep down, didn't want to be dominated by anxiety or be in pain. While we can be the source of much of our own pain, even to the point of creating a prison of depression, it just doesn't make sense. Tim's words describe this paradox. 'Heart never wants to be in pain or anxiety or panic attack. Mind for some reason does. The body was last to show up.'

As we have looked at in evolutionary terms, the body cannot differentiate between a real external threat and an imaginary one in the mind. At the biological level of releasing hormones like adrenaline and activating the stress response in the body, a thought has the same effect on the body as a real threat. Hence the need to break the mind/body connection between thoughts and physical responses. Mindfulness creates the conditions to respond rather than react unconsciously. In effect it creates a gap between the perception and the response or reaction.

At the heart of mindful walking is well-being. Well-being flourishes from the mental and physical posture we take in life. Well-being is about our attitude. Letting go can often be the hardest thing. What sets Tim apart is that he was, despite his doubts, willing to keep walking, step by step, and get the full benefits of mindful walking. This was essentially letting go. He was also finally willing to really listen in silence to the echo of his own opinions and mental distortions, and free himself from the need to believe them. Our thoughts always pass but the emotional echo of those thoughts can return from time to time.

What happened on the mountain that day and in the weeks that followed? We can't know exactly, but in effect, mind and brain, body and nervous system, and the wider context around were given the time and space to work together in the way they were intended.

THE CANDLE AND THE SEA SQUIRT

The metaphor of a candle can be used to enlighten, as it were, the complex interactions of the human mind and nervous system. Running through the candle (the body) is a wick (our spinal cord), the top of which (our brain) can be lit. The aura radiated by the whole candle when alight (the brain/body nervous system working together) can be compared to the powerful mechanism of the human mind. The human mind is hard to define but this gives us one image of its power and complexity.

It all makes sense when you think of why we were given a brain in the first place – as we mentioned, it was to promote or suppress movement. In my teaching I often ask that question of students. The regular response is 'to solve problems' or 'to survive' or 'to self-actualise.' Well, yes and no. These are some of the reasons but, contrary to what you might suspect, the brain was not designed to do any of these things exclusively.

The brain and body and the nervous system originally evolved to control movement. The story of the sea squirt provides a case study. Sea squirts have both male and female organs. They are hermaphrodites. After about three days they develop into a tadpole-like creature. At this time they are endowed with a brain and a nervous system and they behave much like the free-swimming tadpole, wriggling and moving around for a short while until eventually, they settle down and anchor themselves to a rock where they spend the rest of their days.

An amazing transition then takes place. They need to feed, and they proceed to eat their brain and nervous system which was the basis for their early movement. Now that there is no longer a need to move, there is no need for a brain or nervous system.

The brain, as it applies to higher-order animals, is really only relevant for either driving future movement or preventing it. Therein lies the importance of walking and movement, and its centrality to managing our performance.

The brain plays its very important part in all of this. It is now understood, though not completely, that the structure of the brain influences the mind and the mind is not just the activity of the brain.

The mind itself can actually change the structure of the brain. This is the premise of neuroplasticity, which suggests that as the mind changes, the brain changes. To use the metaphor of electrical impulses, it boils down to 'what fires together wires together.' Whatever we choose to focus the mind and our attention in full mindful awareness has an impact on the inner workings of our brain and wider nervous system. This, in turn, affects our emotions and bodily sensations with significant and positive consequences for our performance and well-being. Mindful walk and talk, and sometimes no talk, holistically incorporate the full power of the human make-up.

This all has profound implications. At no cost, we can all take time to walk and focus our attention. There is always choice and the possibility of a better way forward. But you must also accept the present. You are where you are. It is what it is. You are thinking what you are thinking and feeling what you are feeling. Your behaviour is as it is. The big question is, to what degree is any or all of this serving you well? What are the consequences of continuing what you do? However many times you have failed, there is always learning. However difficult the current situation is, there is always possibility, there is always choice, there is always ambition and a better way of viewing and doing. No magic wands here either.

Could it be better? Well, only you can answer that. Are there obstacles? For sure there are. However, there is one certainty, that if you keep repeating the patterns, the rules, the beliefs of yesterday, you will keep getting the results of today. We must try new things to avoid paralysis. As Albert Einstein succinctly put it, 'Insanity:

doing the same thing over and over again and expecting different results.' What needs to change? Could a more mindful approach to your life make a difference? What would that look like? Only you can find out. Only you can begin the experiment.

Mindfulness is about hitting the pause button in your life when you wish. Perhaps now is a good time to pause and reflect. What are you learning from all of this? What is it meaning to you? How could you begin to apply the learning in practical ways? Now might be a good time to capture all of this in your diary. In making a decision to develop your mindfulness practise with walking as its central pillar, there are a number of questions to be answered first.

- Can you do it? The answer is surely 'yes', if you choose to just walk. It may take some extra time, knowledge and training to prepare to take on a more challenging walk such as Tim completed, but we must start small.

- Is this likely to work? You will never know what this will do for you unless you take the first step. This is about an attitude where, in spite of your uncertainty and fears, you take action. It takes self-belief and a willingness to learn from the challenge itself. You may learn to respond positively and proactively to the challenge you have set yourself. That is mindful learning in action.

- Is it worth it? Everything you do is because you have a need to be fulfilled. A journey of self-discovery is always worth it; from earliest civilisation, the ancient Greeks said, 'Know thyself.' In answering these questions you are more likely to build competence and confidence. You inspire yourself to take the first step. Let each step carry the attitude of mindfully moving forward.

'Until one is committed, there is hesitancy, the chance to draw back, always ineffectiveness. Concerning all acts of initiative (and creation), there is one elementary truth that ignorance of which kills countless ideas and splendid plans: that the moment one definitely commits oneself, then Providence moves too. All sorts of things occur to help one that would never otherwise have occurred. A whole stream of events issues from the decision, raising in one's favour all manner of unforeseen incidents and meetings and material assistance, which no man could have dreamed would have come his way.' W.H. Murray.

'Whatever you can do, or dream you can do, begin it. Boldness has genius, power, and magic in it. Begin it now.' Goethe.

5

MINDFUL WALKING IN ACTION

We've hopefully by now explored a little, in our own time, how different meditation postures can help us to develop a particular focus, to set the foundation of calmness and tranquillity. By practising sitting meditation, we can learn how to focus the breath in the present moment.

Mindful walking takes us out of that quiet space, and to a stage of greater insight into what our place is in the extended environment at this time. The practise can root itself in a deeper wisdom, as we come to understand how we fit into that wider external environment and community. In effect we are letting go of some of the internal mental content of our experience, rearranging the internal furniture of our minds and opening up the space around us. To do that we need to get reconnected.

LET GO OF YOUR PAIN

Walking is a stimulating activity. It has an incredible power to uplift and transform the mood. Bring a mindful focus to it and you have a potent mix to calm and empower you. To walk mindfully is to come alive, to be healthy in mind and body. To be fully present in this moment is to be truly present for the next moment, whatever it brings. It is to be truly prepared. In mindfulness we can develop strength, endurance, concentration and clarity. Mindfulness cultivates a mental and physical composure which is the basis of a mental and physical toughness in the face of our unfolding experience.

Toughness, in the mindful sense, doesn't mean being hard or rigid or inflexible. In fact it is quite the opposite. Like branches of a tree we can soften and bend in the strong wind and when the wind has lessened and passed, quickly regain our shape and form. We adapt and lean into life. Mindful walking as a discipline can build this mental and physical toughness, one step at a time. It is the magic of mind and body working in unison, as with just a little more effort every day, great progress is made. One hundred yards, five hundred yards, one kilometre, ten kilometres, they all require the simple act of moving one step at a time.

Mindful walking brings us out of our heads to our real home, our body. In a world where the intellect is prioritised, from our schools to our colleges and workplaces, it is no wonder that we can get caught up with our thoughts. Noticing what is going on in the body in movement and the sensations associated with it is to open us up to the full range of our experience. It is so important to consciously live that experience.

When we draw our attention to bodily sensations we are present in the here and now. In the body there is no yesterday or tomorrow to feel. Try to remember a time when you felt significant physical pain. It is hard to remember or 're-feel' the physical pain of yesterday. If you cut your finger with a sharp knife, the brain perceives this from impulses carried through the nervous system to the brain. That pain exists only in the now, this moment. While the pain may persist for a while, it will inevitably pass.

Memory is different. No nerves are involved in memory. You can memorise the words you are now reading but unless you have the book in front of you, you will never see the original words again. Yes, we can remember the emotional content of the physical pain experienced at a particular point in time, but that also degrades over time. In the body there is only now to feel.

While the present moment is always the only moment we have, the nature of mind is that it tends to overlay past and future as part of the process. Learning to be in the moment gives us the agency to choose which overlay best fits at any time. Choosing that overlay can bring us alive to the present moment or future possibility. Some of us wish that we had some additional weight in our minds to prevent our attention from wandering and heading off like a balloon at times. The weight in our bodies has a grounding effect as it locates us fully in the world we inhabit. It is an effect that the mind could sometimes learn from. We can teach it to ourselves. Even when standing, momentarily bringing a mindful attention to the body and the solid earth beneath it has this grounding effect.

The body thinks also. That is because along with the brain, it is part of the nervous system. It unconsciously experiences feelings and moods. In becoming more aware of this, we can develop better ways of responding to the challenges we face in life, and not reacting too quickly. Hypochondria sufferers often believe that any uncomfortable sensation in the body signals an impending problem. They interpret normal bodily sensations (breathing, heartbeat) or minor physical abnormalities (skin blemishes) or sensations (headaches, stomach aches) as dangerous. They fixate on myriad improbable dangers. They ruminate on what might be wrong. This is just one way in which we can get caught, living in our heads. For some it can be painful. In developing a more mindful relationship with the body we can be with our experience, painful or otherwise, without scrutinising ourselves and catastrophising our futures. We can react less.

A THING OF BEAUTY

Much of the time we don't appreciate the exquisiteness of the body, the splendour of free movement. It is only when we are confined or unwell that we may realise the miracle that is our ability to move our limbs and walk from place to place, the extraordinary skill this involved when we took our first, baby steps. We can take all this for granted. We do so much with our bodies without really appreciating the wonder of carrying, placing, touching, turning, speaking, tasting, smelling. Despite the rapid technological change humans are masterminding, we cannot yet replicate movement in computers that comes anywhere near the complexity of human movement. Computers can replicate the brain with an artificial intelligence that can beat the best of us at chess most of the time, but not the magical movement of gifted footballers.

Some footballers seem to be able to suspend time and space in how they can automatically calculate elevation, distance and power and negotiate any obstacles and interference in between to place a ball where they wish. In the moment, mind and body are working together in perfect synch to calculate the next best step. Putting one foot in front of the other involves no less complexity and is no less exquisite when we walk mindfully.

Anyone who has climbed to the top of a mountain, however high, knows the sensational joy of that moment. It is the magic of living, breathing, being connected. When we walk mindfully we are opening ourselves to the joy of that moment without the clouds of dark thoughts that can sometimes appear when we are motionless, absorbed in ourselves. It is to feel the freedom of the summit, at sea level or wherever you find yourself, moment to moment. The body is magic. Movement is magic.

In mindfulness, the postures of sitting, lying and standing are simple, refined postures. The walking posture, as it moves from stillness into action, is more complex and less refined. There is a lot more muscular input and a lot more happening around us to potentially distract and disturb. We can lose our footing, and we can meet the unexpected. This can be challenging as we begin to walk mindfully. Sensory distractions like sounds and sights can interfere. In adopting a mindful approach to the flux we can face when we walk, we can adopt what we call a 'kinaesthetic awareness.' This is a full-body sensory skill that knows where we are in the space we occupy. We know where our arms and legs and hands and feet are. It sounds simple, but when we are stressed, we can be lacking in this, and are at greater risk of accidents. With kinaesthetic awareness, the nervous system and nerve receptors send messages to the brain to deliver this information. Unless we mindfully focus on the body in the space we inhabit, much of this body experience is unconscious to us and outside our awareness. Walking in the stillness of mindfulness brings this kinaesthetic experience into being.

NOW WALK THE WALK

There is an old Zen saying which goes, 'Stillness in action. Action in stillness.' While practise is central to mindfulness, it is also the most difficult aspect of mindfulness. The beauty of mindful walking is that the practise comes so naturally to us. Movement is such a fundamental part of our lives that we can incorporate informal mindful walking practise into almost every facet of our lived experience.

Pace is an important element of mindful walking. It is important to adopt a pace that allows us to notice the physical experience of walking and the breath. Step by step, not too slow and not too fast. Occasionally as you walk, bring your attention to the body. Recall your breath. Listen to the rhythm of your exhalations, your inhalations. There is no right experience. It is what it is.

It might be as simple as lift, place, set, straighten knee and follow through. Don't take this remarkable mechanism for granted. It was only when walking with Sherpa people in the Nepali Himalayas one day that I discovered how I was unnecessarily wasting energy as I walked on the tops of my toes as I climbed. This was against the background of increasing altitude and diminishing oxygen. My Sherpa walking companions kindly pointed this out to me at one of our rest stops. They showed me how I tended to put all of my weight on the front of my feet as I moved forwards and upwards. 'Relax when you walk,' one said. 'Slowly! Slowly!' laughed the other. (The words sounded like 'Poly! Poly!')

So, going back to the most primitive steps, I suggest to you: Lift leg, place foot, set foot solidly, deliberately straighten knee (especially if climbing) and follow through. One step at a time, slowly, slowly. When you walk, imagine this is a marathon, not a sprint. Take it easy. That way, as you go, you can focus on the full-body sensations of walking, and notice your surroundings.

If something interesting catches your attention, as nature will from time to time, you can always stop and stand and focus. We do this naturally and outside of our awareness. Mindfulness is about bringing intention, focus and an attitude of open curiosity to our actions, including those moments when we pause and stare. Most of the time, while we may stop, we don't fully notice wonderful things, and then we move unmindfully on. With mindfulness, we wake up to our surroundings, absorb the intricacies of nature's design, and create memories worth cherishing.

Early Morning Mindful Walking

Mornings are challenging when it comes to our moods. Some of us wake up renewed and launch into the day like a computer coming back to life, all the previous day's tabs still brightly open.

But often we go through times where we wake up with a sense of lethargy, low energy and little motivation. The intensity can vary depending on the season of the year and the circumstances in our life. Negative moods can root us to the bed and even keep us there, unwilling to budge. The first movement of the day is always to put one foot on the floor. This is magical in its own right. There is a natural stillness in the morning which can be brought to your walking at this time. Let's look at how to begin the day with a mindful walk.

1. First when you wake and while still lying in the bed bring your attention to your breath. Savour and fully appreciate the realisation that it is still working, coming and going. Then bring your attention to your feet. Do a gentle body scan to identify any sensations that are

passing through your body. Maybe there is strain from sleeping awkwardly overnight, or heaviness because you are still stirring awake. When you're ready, place your feet on the floor and feel the touch and textures of being connected to that floor.

2. Now stand up. Continue to focus and notice, breathing in and out in an expansive way, any sensations in this standing position. If your mind tries to take over the peace, notice this too, accept it, and bring the focus back to the breath. No need to hurry yet.

3. Having focused your attention you are now ready to walk mindfully into your day. Maybe that means a walk downstairs to let the dog out, or to the bathroom to brush your teeth and freshen up. Whatever is involved, slow down intentionally. This walk can be done gently and mindfully, and takes very little time. Notice each step of the stairs as you plant your foot and give your body permission to slow down. This mindful beginning sets the tone for the day. Bringing your full attention and presence to these early-morning moments

brings a physical and mental composure to the day ahead. It doesn't mean that you cannot pick up the pace as the day begins, but you do this with more balance. You can also more easily return to a mindful space whenever you require from time to time. Just notice your breath.

4. In doing this meditation, notice how your mood changes. Notice what you are thinking, feeling, experiencing. Has your mood changed in any way since the moment you awoke? It very often has changed, for the better. Notice that too. You can build on this for the day. Brushing your teeth or showering mindfully is all movement, and builds a present mindful simplicity into your day from the start. Your natural generosity of spirit can be part of that simplicity.

MR HAPPY MAN: A MINDFUL WAY

Mindfulness should be simple. In developing

a mindfulness practise we don't have to overcomplicate our life, we just need to show up, focus our attention and be aware of the simple things. Johnny Barnes is an exemplar of mindfulness practise, though he might not have set out to be so. He is now known as Mr Happy Man of Bermuda, recognisable for his bright smile under a straw cap and white beard. For years he worked as a railway electrician, then a bus driver. His retirement brought its challenges. He wondered how he might replace the elements of his working life that gave him meaning. One morning after his retirement he got up at his usual time, prepared a sandwich and a flask of coffee and with a fold-up canvas seat in hand, he headed for the biggest roundabout outside Hamilton, the capital of Bermuda. He was motivated to take up his new job. It had a basic job spec: show up, walk and wish everyone that passed by that roundabout well. He has been there almost every day since, from 5am to 10am.

For the first number of weeks at the roundabout, the feedback from passers-by wasn't very positive. Most people ignored him.

Others shouted abuse at him. He persisted. He kept showing up. The simple things kept happening. Then people got used to seeing him there. Some began to wave back. Their faces grew familiar to him. They told other people about him. People diverted to see this kindly man, who did nothing more than stand around the roundabout and wish people well. No proselytising, just good wishes.

He continued to work at this 'job' he had created. At some point he thought that maybe it wasn't good enough to just give away good wishes. He got a photo of himself printed on a postcard and gave it gratis to people. Generosity and kindness has a power of its own. The wonderful thing about being human is that beyond our insecurities and our initial inability to deal with the new and the strange, we can be very kind. Most people wanted to reciprocate and they did. Johnny Barnes is never short of a Bermudan pound. Every day he continues to show up to his chosen calling.

When people come to know and become comfortable with something, they miss it like a long-time travelling companion when it is not there. They missed Johnny after he went home every morning at 10am. The Hamilton Council solved this, and put up a statue so that Johnny would never be missed. And there is more. He is now the face of Bermudan tourism and is regularly the first Bermudan to meet visiting dignitaries including the Queen of England. In the struggle to make our way in life, how many of us will have a statue put up to recognise our kindness? Johnny Barnes just does the simple things well and with generosity.

UNDOING DESCARTES: 'I MOVE AND I THINK, THEREFORE I AM'

Let us now move on to explore the possibilities of informal mindful walking. Lack of self-belief is the only thing that will now limit the creative development of our new mindful walking practise. There is also the challenge of bringing a focus and a commitment to this new practise. We need to be conscious of what we may be lacking in order to create the intention to practise.

We spend a lot of our time doing. In all the modern-day busyness we take on, the emphasis is on thinking and problem-solving, being in our heads, not physical, manual doing. The education system prepares us for this internal struggle and the wider financial system rewards those who can do it well. With that, technology is increasingly reducing the need for physical doing.

In early childhood, exploration and activity at every sensory level are encouraged. Then as young people grow up, they are asked to sit behind tables for protracted periods of time and absorb a lot of information so as to ultimately demonstrate how good their memory is in exams. This continues into higher education for those of us inclined or lucky enough to get there.

René Descartes was a French philosopher and mathematician, and a leading light in the Western scientific revolution of the 17th century. His insights have informed modern education. His famous saying, 'Cogito, ergo sum', 'I think, therefore I am', placed an overwhelming emphasis and importance on rational, analytical, objective, scientific thinking, where a thinking mind can describe an objective reality. In Descartes' logic, the mind and body are distinct, the body almost just a vessel for conveying the brain around.

While Descartes' theories have advanced the scientific thinking of the last three centuries – he is accepted as one of the fathers of modern mathematics–it has come at a cost. For Descartes, in effect the mind and body were separated in two, as if they coexist independently. This has been discredited as a false dualism, but it has impacted on much post-Enlightenment thinking. In medicine, the medical model of diagnosis and treating the symptoms grew to pre-eminence, without an overall holistic appreciation of the human condition. The approach was: diagnose it and fix it. Rather than advising us to take care of ourselves, and prevent ourselves from needing diagnosis in the first place.

In science it was a question of breaking the problem down into its component parts so as to understand how they fit and work together. For example, an aeroplane is made up of many interrelated working parts. We need to understand the flaws of an aeroplane in case it crashes, and science teaches us to break it into its working parts to do this. But breaking the human mind down into its working parts in order to understand it doesn't always capture the richness and complexity of that mind.

Even in the science of psychology, for many decades, mental health was also a matter of diagnosing negative states of mind like depression and anxiety. With the emergence in the last 10 years of positive psychology, this imbalance is being redressed. There is an increasing acceptance that psychology is not just about mental health problems but also how we can move on to embrace happiness in our lives.

Descartes' dualism was a significant move away from the understanding of the likes of Aristotle. In Aristotelian logic, the mind/body connection, called 'monism', was the basis for understanding the human condition. This approach recognised the unity of the whole person and the complex interaction at physical, mental and emotional levels. How we think, feel and act in the world needs to be understood not in parts but in a holistic way. Descartes' error was to forget the wisdom of the body and how its movement can tell us things. Perhaps it might more usefully have read, 'Ego movere et cogito, ergo sum'. 'I move and I think, therefore I am'.

A GREAT UNKNOWN

Mindful walking is about a particular way of being, with a thinking, conceptual mind of ideas, and thoughts and plans and memories and judgements about all of these passing thoughts all interacting. In journeying through some of the mountains and valleys of our internal mental landscape we may become lost or stuck. Beyond a necessary understanding and acceptance of the way in which we explain our worlds and our place in it, we can be too self-conscious and self-absorbed. The challenge is to get out of our heads, take a break from our heavy, recurring thoughts and get mind and body working together.

You have read half-way into this part of the journey. It is now time to really put mindfulness into action and walk to places not yet considered. Let's first clarify something. Walking is walking. You don't have to leave the comfort of your own home or garden to enjoy mindful walking, and incorporate it into mindful doing. Hiking is walking too, but for longer distances and often in remote locations. Whether mindfully walking the neighbourhood or mindfully hiking the highways and byways of the external landscape, the experience can be rich and varied. There are streets out there you will see differently. There are mountains there to transform your outlook. If mental activity is the default setting of the human mind, then movement is the default position of the human body. Mindful walking is the place where mind and body come together. They inform and pace each other: as the mind tells the body when to halt or rest, the body tells the mind to calm its activity, and take a break. Developing a mindful practise while walking can transfer into your everyday life.

Do try this at home. It's easy to forget that encounters with nature are not just for the countryside. You can listen to birdsong and notice the light on the blades of grass in a mindful way while walking in your back garden, strolling through the local park. You can stop and stare and even examine a wildflower; pick it, get your hands muddy. Pick up new sensations. What do you notice? The experience involves a reckoning with the sounds, smells, sensations and tastes of our wider experience. It is a radical broadening out of who we are.

Nature in the Flesh

Maghnaboe (Macha na mBó in the Irish language), literally translated as 'The Pasture of the Cows', is a glaciated valley surrounded by high vertical mountainous walls on three sides. It is situated on the breathtaking Dingle Peninsula in west Kerry. At the head of the valley three tremendous waterfalls crash down together to feed a river which meanders through the makings of oxbow lakes all the way to the sea in Brandon Bay. St Brendan may himself have walked along this ancient trading route on his way to Killarney or further south.

Maghnaboe is wilderness replete with stories. If you slow down, you will notice the lazy potato beds that are still marked out from Famine times. One hundred and seventy or so years later they lie idle, still waiting for the plough and the curious mindful eye.

The walk into the headwall from the road is gentle and pleasantly undulating. Observing the manner in which people negotiate the early stages of this path can be very revealing. Walking betrays personality and character, and gives a sense of how people lead their lives. Some people head on as if the end was in sight and there was something to prove at that finish line. Others hang back as if there was no end to the day. More seem to settle into the walk as if it was to be enjoyed for itself. They move purposefully but turn their heads and look up and down, giving attention to the unfolding vista. Some walk quickly as if they were running away from something, and walking was just another distraction for a busy mind.

Along the way you will pass testimonies to the uncertainties and dangers of life. Some remembrance plaques bear witness to accident and tragedy in this valley. You eventually come upon the deserted village of Maghnaboe which is itself a testament to the changing nature of life. There is much to be learned from this landscape if you slow down and take time to notice.

Just beyond the relic of a Famine village, the walk becomes challenging with a steep incline rising to meet the unsuspecting walker. The pressure begins to come on and it is then that the uninitiated might remember that they do have a body and it is giving them feedback.

In every walk there is a tipping point. Do I go on or do I turn back? There can be increasing levels of discomfort, even pain, as the body struggles to get the measure of the challenge. It is then that you see how the walker engages with challenge, maybe even with life. It is then that the ego presents itself for inspection.

The mental chatter begins. 'Why did I decide to do this anyway? It's stupid. It's a waste of time.' 'I blame myself for agreeing to it in the first place.' 'I blame him for forcing me into this silly plan.' Anxiety can take over. 'Where is the top? I'll never get to the top.' 'I'm just no good at this. I'm not able.' 'Look at the rest of them; it's so easy for them.' We night even change our rhetoric. 'This is not going to beat me. I must get to the top. I have to get to the top, even if it kills me. Keep the head down. Plough on just in case I get distracted. No need to stop.' Listen to all this mental chatter. Be aware of it. This is like an internal war as we struggle on.

Just as there is a pattern in the landscape, there is a pattern in your own human landscape. Much of it is 'away in the head.' Are you aware of what your inner landscape looks like? What are you walking towards or away from anyway? In this entire struggle you miss a lot.

In this life we need to slow down sometimes. We need to get out of our head at times, especially when we believe everything that is in our head, as we sometimes start to do. We need to rest and replenish. We need to be. The walk can teach us that. Slowly, slowly, one step at a time.

In being open to the whole physical adventure of our body as it moves we can deal more effectively, more mindfully, despite the mental chatter and habitual commentary in our head. We can keep putting one foot in front of another. Who knows where we will end up?

~

6

MINDFUL WALKING IN SPECIAL PLACES

'One may be surrounded by great beauty, By mountains and fields and rivers, But unless one is alive to it all, one might just as well be dead.' Jiddu Krishnamurti'

As alluded to earlier, there is only our imagination to limit us when it comes to walking mindfully in special places. But we can always be imaginative in the places we choose to mindfully walk. Each one of us has a favourite place or places where we find the connectedness that nourishes us. Wherever that place is, why not go there this week and begin your own mindful walking practise. Whether that is in the woods, on your favourite beach, or just through city streets, you can bring the same qualities of mindful noticing to your present-moment experience of these special places. You have it as a gift right now to come alive to your special place. Even if you are not physically there, you can always use the immense power of the brain to take a virtual mindful walk.

As a starting point, this virtual walk that follows might appeal to anyone who might be somewhat lazy when it comes to physical activity. I had a friend once who humorously threatened to set up a new group called 'Athletes Anonymous.' He said it was a group that guaranteed that in the event of any thought of physical activity coming to mind, he could have someone around in five minutes to talk him out of it.

This virtual walk could certainly appeal to those of us who, because of illness or incapacity, are unable to walk. As with every suggestion in this book it is an invitation to experiment in a different way. Play with the power of the mind yourself. This can be very helpful in understanding the distinction between the thinking and non-thinking mind as described earlier.

A Mindful Virtual Walk

1. Find a quiet place to sit down. Bring the focus of your attention to the body and the breath. The body is always in the now. You are always breathing in the now. As you sit and decide to do this, hopefully you are noticing a calmness arising. This exercise in taking an imaginary walk invites you to focus on an actual walk that you may be familiar with. It invites you to create the experience yourself and become the thinker of your thoughts. You are the projectionist in charge of this movie in your head. You project the images and experience the bodily sensations of walking virtually in your favourite place. You can begin to notice also the sensations arising as you proceed on this imaginary virtual walk.

2. Move your attention to the starting point of the walk. Begin to notice where you are. Can you visualise what is around you? What sensations are you noticing in your body? What emotions are you aware of?

What thoughts are you aware of? For me, I can picture cars parked in the car park above Cloghane village in west Kerry at the start of the climb to Brandon Mountain. I can picture a weather-beaten sign offering mountain craft advice to the would-be climber. I have a sense of the stones under my feet as I adjust my walking poles. I can feel the excitement in my stomach of returning to what I call the 'source.' My special place. Very soon I come to the first gate and cross the small stream. I am there. I can hear the sound of running water.

3. As you begin this virtual walk, trace your footsteps. Can you describe the underfoot conditions? Can you try to piece together the changes that are occurring as this movie unfolds? What are the colours and shapes around you? These are only thoughts and memories but they are powerful in the effect they can have on the body. The body might have no real idea of whether they are real or in this case imagined. It reacts to the

imagery you are remembering or creating in greater detail. Visualising positive, personally meaningful images can change our mood. Visualising is about taking charge of your thought process. Instead of being in some way driven by your thoughts you create them. You are in charge. For me, visualisation finds practical application when at times I find myself awake in the middle of the night ruminating about some issue or other. I begin to focus on my favourite place and walk on, only to wake up some time later.

4. The virtual walk can be as long as you wish. The intention in this exercise is to develop a practise where you take control of the thinking process. This is visualisation not mindfulness. This is clearly different to mindfulness where you do not set out to control your thinking, you just observe it.

5. If this exercise touched you, briefly make a note in your diary and try to capture as best you can what you noticed, where it has left you.

MINDFULNESS: A CATCH-ALL PLACE TO BE

If you have started thinking of special places you'd like to walk in, there are surely places that immediately spring to mind. But the power of mindfulness is that you can make every place that you find yourself in special. This is because, in suspending the judging conscious and unconscious mind, you come to see something different and special before you. At mindfulness, every place becomes special in the moment. Those moments frame the future in a more positive, empowering and calming way. The interesting thing about this practise we call mindful walking is that it facilitates the development of qualities we already have, wherever we find ourselves. These are the qualities and foundational attitudes of mindfulness that can always at any time be brought to the walk.

MY MORNING SUNRISE

Mindful walking first and foremost requires us

to bring attention to the body. As the medieval poet Rumi wrote, 'Just being sentient and in a body with the sun coming up is a state of rapture.' It is to be alive to the moment. One morning, I was of a part with Rumi as I walked to the beach.

A coastal haze hung over Tralee Bay as the sun made its predictable glowing emergence to the east. There was no storyline except the captivating display on view before the real business of the day began. Even the mechanical drone of a distant fishing boat didn't take from the ability to be fully present. That drone was noticed non-judgingly. The day was revealing itself as every day does, in its own time.

It seemed a little easier that morning to become attuned to my breathing and other senses. Perhaps it was because I had made a silent commitment when I woke that day, to spend some quiet moments with moving, touching, seeing, hearing, stepping and tasting.

I stood for a moment. I closed my eyes and in the distance I heard the sound of a crowing pheasant. It was as if my breathing was drawing those beautiful sounds into my body. That game bird passed, only to be replaced by the sound of a cuckoo. It was suddenly soothing; I couldn't think why. My body knew this. It was connected and giving me a message of ease, contentment and peace. There was no attempt to judge the sound I was hearing as good or bad. It just was.

I listened more closely, standing still, as the noise petered away. I returned to the breath and opened my eyes. The sun had now disappeared behind a cloud. A momentary attachment arose. 'I hope it returns soon.' I caught myself in this grasping thought. It passes, I remembered. I refocused my attention. 'I am not moving,' I resolved. I stood in silence listening to this early-morning world. Nature has a way of drawing us in if we let it. It was truly beautiful at that moment. I had to wipe away a tear. That's ok too, I decided.

What needs to happen for us to pull back the curtain more often, to see the sunrise? I learned what needs to happen from this walk. You probably only have to walk a short distance to pull back the curtain, and let the light in. The mystery of mindfulness in the morning is waiting for you.

In special moments like that morning, self-centred thinking and relentless 'doing' seem to fade away. It is a rare realisation which is hard to catch at the level of the thinking mind, which just wants to put it in a category: good or bad. When we become truly connected to our senses, we notice and really see things as they are. In being one with our surroundings, the ego seems to evaporate like steam. It is to transcend the tawdry limitations of a 'self', centred on its own small, narrow agenda. To be fully present in the moment is to forget ourselves and in so doing, become part of a bigger picture of possibility. There is no moment except this moment of experience.

A Mindful Non-Judging Day

The attitudes of mindfulness can be explored one by one. Mindfulness is not to set aside the judging part of the mind, because this is impossible. It is to become more attuned to it and notice the sometimes unmindful routines and patterns we tend to get entangled in very quickly. We can judge and react quickly, and overreact. For us all at times, the gap between the thought and the word, the mind and the mouth is much too narrow. We have the thing said before we give ourselves time to actually think. Developing a strategy to notice the patterns that form in us makes space for a response, not a reaction. It makes more space for more options and a better knowledge of the situation. Take some time today to slow down and notice your style of judging.

The Field

As Frank walks to the car the air is fresh on his nose. He deliberately focuses on his breath. He's excited and hopeful. He hasn't had this sense of childhood excitement in a long time. It's in fact well over 40 years since he has felt so open to possibilities.

He has an underlying uncertainty. His friend Seán, the local farmer, had told him he would find what he came for. But he thinks to himself, 'I know he told me I'd find some, but how could it be? I thought agricultural fertiliser had put paid to all of that.' The self that remembers can be excited and hopeful but also uncertain and distrusting.

Frank catches himself in the midst of this familiar narrative of competing thoughts and emotions. He drives on, focusing mindfully, to his destination. Next to him in the passenger seat is the cardboard box he placed there the night before, which he intends to fill. He senses the anticipation now in his stomach. He knows he is here in this very moment. It is special.

When he arrives at the roadside gate, he sets out to slow down, to walk and explore with interest. Without effort, he is once again both back with his father at a similar gate, and also alone with himself in the present moment. Now in his aloneness there is a lingering sadness. He wishes his father could be there.

It is amazing that we can be both here and there at once. The volume of the dawn chorus soundtrack seems to grow and interrupt. Frank notices. He is in touch with what he is doing and he is in touch with himself also. There is a 'being' to his 'doing' this morning.

A weighted lack of confidence still moves with him, his eyes straining to remember what the thing he was searching for should look like. As he walks slowly, he scans the dew-covered grass in front of him. When will that memory, the imagined mental picture from 40 years ago, match the real thing? The self that remembers and the self that experiences struggle together. And then he sees one. It is real. It is not a memory. Past and present melt into one.

He slowly bends down, and as he had learned with his father all those years before, cups his hand around the stem of the mushroom and lifts it. After 40 years, it is as if it was the very first one he had ever picked. The exquisite softness and pristine whiteness of the cap engrosses him. He turns it over to inspect the brown gills, symmetrical and perfect. He takes time. A wish that he could have shown it to his father comes and goes. That was not possible.

He lifts it to his nose and matches a long-forgotten memory of a real mushroom with the one he holds in his hand. He tastes it like he used to. On the tip of his tongue it carries the very essence of the earth from which it came.

He is here. He has caught the moment. He is this very moment. But he is also this mental time traveller; he catches himself anticipating once again, imagining what it might be like to fry off that mushroom in butter and cream a little later. He can almost smell and taste that too on lightly toasted and buttered bread.

But then, uncertainty returns. Maybe it's the only mushroom he'll find? He moves on. The farmer was right. Why did he not believe him? He focuses again, and walks mindfully through that field for another hour before returning to his car with mushrooms to share. That's a good feeling too. On this morning, he is in touch with his past, present and future. He is once again a child, free to roam in curiosity, but with the wisdom of years behind him. This is mindful magic.

It is strange, some months later, for Frank to reflect on this mushroom moment in time. In truth, as with much of life, he was just lucky. Were it not for the kindness of his friend the local farmer, who was willing to share his bounty, he would have continued to wonder if he would ever taste a real mushroom again.

Frank had a wonderful experience that day, one that took him back to childhood. It is gone now and maybe never to return but he was lucky to once again have treasured the experience without the need to hold on to it. That morning was open with life. He was up for it, and willing to resist hindrance or interference. He was open to the movements of his mind. He was open to the movements of his body. He was open to what the wild outdoors had in store. Honey emerged from the earth that morning and he really noticed and appreciated it.

The Australian Aboriginals have a word that might describe what happened that morning for Frank: 'walkabout'. Walkabout describes how at certain times of their lives they head off alone into the remote outback and perform rituals; dancing and chanting and rock and body art. For the Aboriginals, performing these rituals unlocks memories and knowledge which become part of their lived personal experience. They contend, without any scientific evidence, that this even extends to unlocking the memories of their ancestors.

Science teaches us that memories don't just reside in the mind or brain. The body can react to a reconstructed memory of past experience too. For Frank, picking mushrooms with his father when he was very young was a ritual of sorts. In mindfully embracing the morning and its potential, moment by moment, Frank unlocked the past such that it was very much part of his present-moment experience. His body felt this too. In the mindless rush of normal life, we can lose this capacity and skill. Slow down, walk slowly. Savour. Appreciate and let the body catch up.

A Mindful Trusting Day

We distrust for very good reasons. We wish to remain safe and to be sure that people won't mislead us. Today as you walk, take some time to slow down and notice how you tend to be distrustful, and in what situations. To notice is to become aware. To become aware is to have choice. To what degree is this serving you well? Is it growing your relationships? If you were to slow down and challenge some of this distrusting of yourself and others, would you be less inclined to judge yourself and others so readily? It is impossible to set aside the untrusting element of our make-up. But we can work to be as certain as we can before making decisions. This is good. When it tends to be automatic and unconscious it does not leave much room for knowing the full story. There are times when it may be inappropriate to stop and explore the full story, especially when there is real danger about. However, we often distrust and react more rapidly than may be beneficial, even when there is no real danger. Today, explore your own style mindfully and see more clearly.

The City Flâneur

For those of us who live in a bustling capital, walking around the city is taken for granted. We can forget that in the city, just wandering about can be most pleasurable. The French even have a word for it. A 'flâneur' is a stroller, someone who ambles and wanders on without apparent purpose.

Susan Sontag called the city a 'landscape of voluptuous extremes'. If mindful walking alerts us to the amazing adventure that is life, walking mindfully around our city can alert us to the amazing background to our life. As a potential mindful flâneur, we can bring our attention to this urban landscape as we wish, and enjoy the novelty of looking up and sideways at times. I see this as a rich form of mindful wandering. The designer Alan Fletcher in his book *The Art of Looking Sideways* describes it as observing without purpose:

'Flâneurs don't have any practical goals in mind, aren't walking to get something, or to go somewhere. What flâneurs are doing is looking. Opening their eyes and ears to the scene around them, wondering about the lives of those they pass, constructing narratives about the houses, eavesdropping on conversations, studying how people dress and street life in general. Flâneurs relish what they discern and discover.'

This description does point to the possible interruptions of perambulating the urban landscape with a beginner's mind, watching the comings and goings, the ins and outs. The noise is a challenge to mindfulness when we are searching for deeper contemplation but nonetheless it links the rhythm of our bodies and minds with the background setting. The background we live with can always be observed and attended to, non-judgingly and with curiosity. While the smells and noises of the city can be at times offensive, distracting and challenging, the city is in effect only another arena in which to notice and to develop our mindful practise. We can go where we want on foot, but slow down and stop, as if to get to know the terrain for the first time and our place in it.

We tend to be conditioned and habituated to the clamour of the city. We take it for ordinary: the sound of passing cars, people walking by. It is only when we notice the silence of the countryside that we fully appreciate how intrusive this can all be. To listen mindfully to this particular soundtrack, beyond distraction, is to find yourself. It is to come to rest in what is, without labelling it good or bad, pleasurable or not. It is to observe without becoming attached.

I recently met a foreign visitor to my city while out walking. He had discovered more in a short walk than I had in almost sixty years. He had taken the time to look up. Even in some derelict buildings he could see the history of colour and shape and shadow. As he shared his infectious insights, enthusiasm and energy with me, I couldn't help but become aware that this mindfulness knows no bounds. No matter how long we practise there is more to be seen.

This gentleman had never heard of mindfulness. I did enquire politely. He told me he just had a natural capacity for childlike curiosity. We all have these qualities if we can shift beyond the preoccupations of the judging mind.

Despite the noise, we can clear our head in the city too. Some day we will be immobile and unable to do this. Why not then walk more, learn more, savour more the sights, the sounds, the smells of your city. Appreciate more. You always have the choice.

A Mindful Beginner's Mind Day

To be childlike is to be alive. To be alive is to be carefree, playful and innocent. It is a gift. Our life may have brought us to a place of pain, cynicism, negativity, or know-it-all certainty and arrogance. We may have spent many years trapped by our view of the world and unwillingness to explore with a different mindset. To be curious is to be spontaneous and open. It is to be open to celebrate life in a fresh and different way. This gift can only be unwrapped in the present. The well-being and happiness and contentment that come from this gift do not arise from searching for other gifts elsewhere. If we can somehow learn that the present is the only gift we have then we may know the power of mindfulness and mindful walking in our lives. We may come to realise that searching for material gifts or instant gratification provides only short-term reward. The shine of any recently bought item soon wears off. We get tired and bored and then we move on. Today, as you go about your life, slow down and try to look with different eyes. What are you missing? Go beyond the initial judgement of good or bad. Go beyond the initial distrust to discover the new. Just go beyond the assumption or rule or belief you hold about the experience. What does going beyond it bring? It might be as simple as listening to really hear. The joy and happiness that can come from being alive and, in this case, alive to your city and the people of the city is a true gift that you can unwrap every day.

~

ON THE HILLS AND MOUNTAINS

In her book *Eight Feet in the Andes*, the Irish travel writer Dervla Murphy writes, 'But I know and have always known that human beings need to escape at intervals from the alien world which has so abruptly replaced the environment that bred us. We need to be close to, and opposed to and sometimes subservient to and always respectful of, the physical realities of the planet we live on.'

The city is the 'alien' if interesting world that

now contains us. But remote places are what bred us and they continue to attract us. Away from the bluff and bluster of the city, remote places have special meaning for us. There is richness in nature which draws us mysteriously towards it. We cannot deny it despite the constraints modern living puts on us. Getting out of town on a regular basis should not be a luxury, it is a need.

Exiting busy urban atmospheres can be essential to our unwinding. But we must not deny ourselves access to the beauty that's out there waiting. Going for mindful walks on the hills and the mountains is to creatively use your exterior adventures to grow confidence and resilience within. Well-being, happiness and peace strengthen in this process.

Mindful walking in the great outdoors is a challenge, of course. There are risks and inherent uncertainty in going to places remote and unknown, even if they are signposted and paved. Remote places are far outside the comfort zone we've become used to. But in experiencing new challenges and developing new strategies to solve problems, there is a sense of accomplishment in every walk. The benefits of mindfully walking outside the comfort zone arise in your thinking, emotions and behaviour. There is always the possibility of the mindful walker making a connection between the adventure of walking in remote places and real life. A sense of 'Yes, I can feel the fear and do it anyway.'

Wild and remote landscape appeals to our connectedness to something bigger than ourselves. Traversing the great undulating 'stone book' of remote places brings us closer to explaining things we find hard to explain. The meaning of it all, where we fit into the great order of things. If nothing more philosophical, it calms the mind and lets us be at ease with the unknown. There can be a complete letting go. It also nourishes the 'being' through physical 'doing.'

To walk mindfully, high up in nature, is to feel the world and your place in it with a freshness that is energising, empowering and calming. It can take you to a state of profound contemplation. In travelling to remote places your sense of self comes together in both an enhanced and diminished way. You remember your smallness in the universe. The mountain can, of course, be tough at times, but there is an outer spaciousness that mirrors an inner spaciousness.

The natural world has a way of keeping us in our place and slowing us down. We have to adapt to it. It is then that we can appreciate the moment, the now and the centrality of our body to our experience and performance.

The ego can see its insignificance in the great order of things. The mountain top brings mind, body and environment together. On good days it might even be called 'spiritual' in that otherworldly blend that happens: we are not on the mountain, we *are* the mountain.

Can you try to define what is so special about mountains? Our everyday language of 'doing' is replete with the metaphor of the mountain: 'peak experiences', 'peak performance', 'reaching the summit'. Altitude seems to have a humbling effect on us. Much psychological research points to the restorative benefits of contact with nature. Mindful walking in remote places allows our mind to drift from one sensory experience to another while we make the time to observe it. Regularly setting ourselves in the wider fabric beyond the slopes of our ambition or urban lifestyle relaxes us. This place of rock, earth, air and water from which we have evolved and which we share with other living organisms facilitates emotional relaxation. In the mountains we can come to know ourselves intimately and just be. We are connected to ourselves, others and nature. Up on high there can be an incredible lightness of being.

Mindful walking invites us to develop increased sensory awareness. Having nothing to do but walk and observe for a day is beyond pleasure. It is like being back in our childhood where the activity was the purpose and it really didn't matter much what the outcomes were. We walk because we walk. We talk because we talk. Walk and talk. Talk and walk. Motion and emotion go comfortably hand in hand even to the edge of awe on occasions.

Friedrich Nietzsche wrote that 'In the mountain of truth, one never climbs in vain, you either reach a higher step today or exercise your strength to climb higher tomorrow.' It is a statement that encapsulates mindfulness. In walking mindfully we don't set out to achieve anything but there are consequences that arise as a result.

Developing resilience in the face of challenge and setback in life is important. On the journey and on the walk, hardiness arises as we deal with challenge and bounce back. The psychologist Albert Bandura describes this resilience of ours as 'self-efficacy.' It's a sense that 'Yes, I can.' The only way that you will ever know if you can is to take the next step. Do it. Nobody said it would be easy but your diary now has the beginnings of any new adventure you choose. This could be a new story for you. Can you now see the challenge as it is and not worse than it is? How can you now see it better than it is? Can you now mindfully make it the way you see it? What more do you need to write to make it real and possible beyond perceived obstacles?

Mindful walking in remote places builds personal resources. With practise it develops both a sense of internal control and a belief that we can jump before we are ready. Paradoxically, this rigour and self-belief entails an acceptance of the fragility of our place in a world where we ultimately have no control. The Tibetan

Buddhist Kalu Rinpoche reminded us that there is a wisdom in letting go when he wrote, 'You live in an illusion and the appearance of things. There is a reality but you do not know this. When you understand this, you will see that you are nothing, and being nothing you are everything. That is all.'

We spend so much of our time trying to be somebody, that to be truly at one with the mountain is to realise that we are nobody, a nothing struggling to cling to a rock. When we spend so much time constructing a sense of self, this is hard to swallow. Bigger business, more qualifications, more stuff, more money and all in an effort to validate one's worth.

It takes courage to accept that you are 'nothing and everything.' Courage comes before confidence. The paradox of accepting that you are 'nothing and everything' allows us to address the important questions. It also facilitates acceptance of the realities of life. We must remind ourselves of the certainties. I am going to die. This walk will end. I am so fortunate to be able to walk. I have nothing to lose really. I can be free from attachment and the power that it exerts over me. I can finally awaken to the fact that there is no fear beyond that which is constructed by me, away somewhere in my own head. The world misleads us when it suggests that we can be free of fear and more secure if we have more or bigger insurance policies.

In going to the mountain we can carry along a veritable personal library of underlying assumptions, beliefs, rules and patterns of thinking, feeling and behaving, both conscious and unconscious. These, as we have seen, can negatively and unwittingly affect how we perceive the present moment of our unfolding experience. Memories come back repeatedly and for some may carry a heavy load of negative emotional energy. We persist in carrying that load, that slight, that offence, what could have been. The rucksack of our lives can be full and heavy and can weigh us down.

The mountain has different ideas. Traversing it is a way of untangling the painful web we may have woven for ourselves. In taking the next step on the mountain the baggage of a lifetime can be observed mindfully and divested from us. In developing a greater internal wholeness and external connectedness, a more meaningful acceptance and sense of self beyond fear can emerge. Fear will never leave us but we can be more accepting of it. Improved self-confidence, responsibility and self-motivation are all expected by-products of the challenge of mindful walking in remote places.

On the mountain, the self-motivated journey to health, well-being and happiness continues as you better understand and deal with your interferences. With a healthy loss of ego the mountains of the mind don't appear so high and better physical and mental fitness follows.

A Mindful Acceptance and Letting Go Day

As we walk we can look on ourselves more kindly and compassionately. We can even smile at ourselves and realise our insignificance. When we shine the light on the grasping ego, it seems to dissolve. If we consider the precariousness of our existence we have a very real choice. Do we continue to struggle against the forces that shape us or do we choose to accept? Accepting means letting go of our grasping and attachments. Letting go does not mean stopping the journey, but rather to do so in greater awareness of what is real. In letting go we become the master and not the servant of our thinking. Becoming the master is about the story you can now write. That story may not bring you to the top of Kilimanjaro, but it surely can bring you to places of greater well-being, happiness and contentment. Letting go of the negative routines and patterns allows us to be alive to the moment, with an energy and spirit that makes anything possible. Today, take some time to mindfully let go and become alive to the possibilities of your life. What is the next chapter of that story? Write it down in your diary to make it come alive. Share that story with someone. Mindfully lean into that story and see what happens.

After Dark

It is now mid-August in the west of Ireland. I am stopped, alone on the Caher Road. It might sound strange. I have no purpose here at night except to be here fully. While it is pitch black, I can still notice things. My night vision, given a chance, is working as it should. I can pick out the shapes all around. I can see that the Perseid meteors are back as they flash across the clear sky like blazing fireworks. These bright meteor showers happen every August and are best appreciated in a dark place like this lonely road I'm standing on. As St Lawrence said, 'Night has no darkness for me, but all things become visible in the light.' My attention is drawn to this wonderful spectacle but what else is visible in the dark? What else can I mindfully notice as I walk slowly?

The dark of the night brings a certain unease but I focus on my breath and each sense in turn. I become more intensely aware of my feelings in this experience. The smell of the honeysuckle. The uneven stones beneath my feet. The fuchsia that seem to glisten in the starlight. I touch the dew. The distinctive flutter and cry of the curlew fades hauntingly across the bog. While I cannot see him, I can feel him. We are one on this beautiful night with no purpose.

I am not the first to hear the curlew, but I can

hear it in my own unique way. I am here in the moment, just myself. There is no sense that I am striving to be anywhere else. There is no sense that I am trying to make it any more than it is. The experience is the knowing. The experience is the connection. The knowing is mindful and mindfulness knows patience.

I wait for a moment, hoping that the spell won't be broken. It is, but I walk on ... noticing the magic of this place and this night. And like everything on this journey, I am at one with the darkness that's around, connected to an inner narrow and wider external reality. That moment too passes. However, I also know that I can come back to this place, even when the lights are bright. I always have my imagination. I celebrate the moment as I turn mindfully for home.

A Mindful Non-Striving Day

The pillars of mindfulness like Trust, Acceptance, Patience, Non-Judging, Non-Striving, Beginner's Mind and even Letting Go make sense to the thinking, conceptual mind. However, for the Western thinking mind conditioned to 'doing' and more 'doing', the notion of 'doing nothing' can be profoundly challenging. We are goal driven. There must be a purpose. Mindful walking is different. It is not about the destination, it is about the journey. There is no goal except to be fully present with yourself on the walk.

If you walk and think to yourself, 'This is going to be a good walk' or 'I have to be first to the top' or 'I have to get fitter' or 'I am going to love the company and be the funniest in the group', then you are already stuck in your 'monkey mind'. There, you cling to the notion that you should be somewhere other than the present moment. There is an underlying assumption that your world is not good enough yet. This is where the pain arises. 'This is not good enough yet.' The paradox is that being in the present without striving to be anywhere else is more likely to deliver on those goals.

Accepting that things are good enough now is to be in the present without needing to be anywhere else. Mindfulness and mindful walking offers an open invitation to sit or stand or lie or walk in that present moment. You are spoilt for choice. There is no purpose other than to be fully in the moment. If you have a sense that you want to be first to the top, investigate that. Peel back the onion and explore what is simply an idea that may be unconsciously driving your behaviour. Observe closely and non-judgementally to really see who or what is driving this particular goal. You always have choice. Do I really wish to make this choice? Experiment with having a mindful non-striving day and capture the freedom of this in your diary. Throughout the day, create some space to do nothing. Intentionally set aside five minutes to do this every day.

Letting go of the need to control is difficult for us all. When you do let go by doing nothing, feel the anxiety, stress, annoyance lift. You have less imaginary worries. The future looks after itself and you are better prepared to deal with the real worries that arrive.

7

MINDFUL WALKING AND TRAVEL

a known route and walk in a group, but try to spend some time walking apart from the group. As the author Lillian Smith noted, you will soon realise that 'no journey carries one far unless, as it extends into the world around us, it goes an equal distance into the world within'.

The embodied experience of walking far from home engages people in different ways. It is fatal to maintain a narrow-minded perspective on life, and travel is one way of broadening your understanding of all kinds of life. That phrase 'to find yourself' might be used in jest but that is what we do abroad, look out in order to look back in, unravel the mystery of who we are. On a long and strange path there can be much time spent alone with ourselves, noticing our unconscious and conscious thoughts. Everything is novel: we can experiment with different scenarios and interpret our experience in different ways. On the walk we can stop and reflect and make new meaning for ourselves. We can stand and stare within and without. We can see ourselves relative to others, and look in deeper. We can belong and share. We can learn the conversation of compassion. On the walk we can at times struggle with our own insecurities and prejudices, and a mindful approach can help us carry on.

THE WAY OF THE PILGRIM: CAMINO DE SANTIAGO DE COMPOSTELA

Mindful walking in any place can change you. It can lay before you a unique understanding of the self. Travelling to mindfully walk and talk will leave impressions on mind and body that polish the experience of your life. I have always found it extraordinary that in travelling to faraway places, we can notice more deeply and with greater fascination what we might tend to ignore at home. Travel teaches us to be mindful of diversity but also the diversity that is outside our front door when we return home.

There are many way-marked routes all over Europe which converge on the city of Santiago in north-western Spain. The Camino Francés (French Way) is probably the most famous of these. This route has featured in many documentaries, books and films and is better known as 'The Way.' It is a walk through stunning landscapes from the vineyards of Rioja, to the open spaces of Meseta, the mountains of León and O Cebreiro and finally the peaceful hills of rural Galicia, before finally reaching the city of Santiago de Compostela.

Its official start point is on the French Basque side of the Pyrenees at St Jean Pied de Port, although many walkers join at different points along the route. The French Way stretches for 790 kilometres. Some people walk the full length of the Camino which could, for the fit and injury-free, take four to seven weeks. Others take it in stages, perhaps a week at a time. Many return year on year to cover different parts of the route.

They say that walking this ancient pilgrim route to Santiago will change your life. People walk the Camino for many reasons. There is no one single factor that brings people to this magical place. It is a tapestry of meanings and stories. This ancient route links mind and body, doing and being, thinking and moving around themes which are foundational for the overall well-being, happiness and peace of the pilgrim walker.

The use of the word 'pilgrim' is not to define the walker in religious or spiritual terms, although religion or spirituality might be important for some in undertaking the walk. Rather, the word pilgrim gives a broader understanding of someone who is mindfully taking time out to review and reflect on the current state of play in their lives. Getting away and taking time out from the daily grind and clutter of modern living brings many of us to the Camino. It is an opportunity to cut out the stasis and background interference of modern life, and distance oneself from what's become ordinary. Many journeys on the Camino are started with a burden of baggage both physical and mental.

In taking on a walk like the Camino you are accepting challenge. You are invited to leave your comfort zone and see how well you are equipped to deal with a new experience. There is a physical challenge also which excites many, terrifies others. 'Will the body hold up?' 'Will the feet serve me well?' 'Will I be able?' you might hear people ask. Over time, you grow into the walk. In getting stronger as you go you become more comfortable and attuned to your body.

There is always the possibility of a new perspective stemming from new encounters and new people. The tension between aloneness and belonging can be reconciled on the walk. Each has its benefits, and on this walk we can undo the tension, and just be – alone among others.

There is a particular sense of focus on this walk, narrowed mostly to the day ahead, with easily identified goals, little route-planning and a decent timeframe to achieve what you hope for. There is always an underlying purpose to the day but it does not weigh heavily, when you are stretching your legs and swinging your arms in this magnificent countryside. A bit like the seasons, the goal emerges in its own good time and as a consequence of a gentle mindful engagement with the process of just walking.

There is of course an element of planning required but the layout and services on the route for the most part make this relatively easy. Most of the walking routes encountered in France and Spain are laid out since medieval times where half a day's walk (15 km or so) brought you to a hamlet for lunch and a full day's walk (30 km or so) brought you to dinner and bed in the late afternoon.

And what a sense of achievement each evening when the next village or town is eventually reached. Arriving at the place you have mapped out that morning fuels confidence and positivity. The evenings bring a time for reflection and review of how the day went. It is an opportunity to make an honest assessment. The natural and mindful contemplation of the walk is nourished by this review and reflection later. Values signpost every step of the Camino. Honesty, simplicity, courage, commitment, humility and awareness pop up when least expected and point to what is important. They add a sustainable purpose over time to the walk.

As the days march on, the journey develops a momentum and energy of its own. It becomes the purpose in itself, with an easy future orientation which sits well with a mindful curious focus on the present moments of the experience. This is where non-striving begins to resonate with you. One step, one moment, no need to strive. It's amazing how they all add up.

You can't fool yourself on the Camino. You have to be honest with yourself. On the walk, you can of course tell others the big story, but when you lie down in your bunk in the refugio at night, you're on your own with your narrative, with your own story. The wondrous thing about a walk of this scale and depth is that you can always rewrite that story, bring a fresh perspective to your life.

Depending on the distances you set yourself, and once the walking is not too physically demanding, you have a lot of time to think. You might start to consider where you have come from and where you are going to, both on the walk and in your life. This walk is a metaphor. 'Look how far I have come,' you might say to yourself. When you look forward in your life, there is, much like the walk, always something untried, somewhere new to go. The rhythm of the walking facilitates this mindful contemplation. It is also very humbling to walk in the steps of others and hear their stories of adversity and resilience.

Walking the Camino is a confirmation of the strange power of simple things in life, like walking and talking. It is about savouring, appreciating and sharing. It fosters a sense of gratitude in you, as each day ends and another is on the horizon with all its possibility. Kindness is encountered in unusual and unexpected places. A kind comment. A positive affirmation shared. One as simple as 'Well done' or 'Keep going' from a fellow traveller. Transition and change are overarching themes on a walk like this. In body, mind and heart, it is about moving on from the previous day. It might also be about moving on from loss, bereavement or retirement. The Camino, for some, involves brief respite from the spinning mind that results from the sudden unexpected loss of a loved one. In each story there are crossroads to be negotiated. The physical act of walking alone in the early mornings brings a sense of balance and relief from the pain. It is cathartic.

A new consciousness can emerge, borne out of the needs that we all have and that are provided for as we walk and talk in a special place. These needs are simple. On the Camino, being part of a group satisfies our need for affiliation. Friendship, support, connectedness. Within, we gain equilibrium, challenge, purpose. These are also the needs that Johnny Barnes lives his daily life by. All you are asked to do on the Camino is show up like Johnny, every morning.

A sense of belonging is what captivates most on the Camino. How often do we really explain or share our feelings honestly? Getting to know a person highlights the power of the social. There is no better way to get to know anyone than to walk with them. The sharing is physical and emotional. Mindful walkers come to a realisation that people are what is important in life. Our stories and the pain we all carry may differ in content and intensity but we share more than what divides us. That support so often missing in lives is given freely. The camaraderie and the bonding can almost be touched. Stories are exchanged on the walk and in the evenings. You start to think, 'My story is not that bad really.' It is humbling. If we are mindful on these encounters, we can become aware of our impact on others. They are as vulnerable as we are.

After a long day's walking and even in the midst of tiredness, there is a natural and sometimes spontaneous fun and enjoyment which emerges unbidden. Sometimes people burst into song and dance with the sheer mind and body freedom and joy that arises beyond inhibition.

The Camino has a long history and heritage. It is a history of sharing and supporting the traveller. The support of a stranger shows just how connected we all are. The journey also shows just how small we really are in the wider context of things. 'There is always something greater than me,' we start to realise. In walking mindfully out here, we can be together in this sharing.

The exquisite pleasure of having nothing else to do each morning when you get up other than to walk mindfully at your own pace for the rest of the day is set against an ever-changing landscape that is wrapped around you as you make your way through it. This is a holiday for mind and body, an extended period of recreation which itself points to the refreshment of mind and body through a stimulating activity like walking.

This is simple, mindful stuff but so easily forgotten the day we return from the Camino. We can be mindful of that too as we plan our next walk. When we return, we must be mindful of what we have learned and consider how we apply it to our life and work experience. Family life requires work. Our work is a place of complex relationships too. Our relationships can be the source of great happiness or pain. We know all too well how they can go wrong and toxic very quickly. In the rush to the bottom line we often forget the importance of relationships and the power of our own conversation to form those relationships. I believe the Camino can teach us in microcosm the value of solidarity with others.

Not all journeys to distant and exotic lands turn out the way one might wish. Adrian's story is testament to the unpredictability and unfairness of life, how life can knock us back and rattle us to the core.

A Soldier's Awakening: Adrian's Story

Life could have turned out quite differently for Adrian, but it didn't. Though as he says himself, 'My life since the incident has been somewhat a disaster but I am still standing here.'

Adrian could have looked at his past and

bemoaned his mistakes, his errors of judgement and behaviour, hurting those close to him. For a long time, his past consumed him. How he has come to remain standing he ascribes in part to an inherited inner strength. The support of others over a space of 30 years has been central to his return to well-being. 'I am now at peace with myself,' he says. Walking alone and in groups has played a central part in his recovery. Adrian's story is not so much about what happened to him on his travels but rather, what he learned from it over time.

In 1980, in a small village high in the hills of Southern Lebanon, while serving with the United Nations Interim Force in Lebanon (UNIFIL), a soldier from Fiji died in Adrian's arms. The village of At-Tiri was the first place Irish troops saw full-scale offensive military action since the Congo in the early 1960s. Following that action, Captain Adrian Ainsworth was, along with others, awarded the Military Medal for Gallantry with distinction, 'for displaying exceptional bravery and compassion of a high order where at At-Tiri on 7th April 1980, with grave danger to his own life from direct and sustained fire, he crawled a distance of 200 metres to aid a grievously wounded comrade and, still under fire on the return journey, brought him to a place of safety'. It is an experience that, hopefully, none of us will ever encounter. Heroes are only human too; they struggle with the same fears as everyone but manage to set those aside in coming to the assistance of others.

It is a reflection of the poor awareness of mental health and well-being at that time that it wasn't until 16 years later that Adrian, having gone through much emotional pain and suffering, was finally diagnosed with post traumatic stress disorder (PTSD) and chronic depression. In the intervening period, he met with other challenges. Bereavement and relationship issues only compounded the trauma of At-Tiri. Adrian was, through no fault of his own, falling into some large unanticipated potholes of negative life experience and while trying to avoid making matters worse, was not doing a very good job of holding things together. He was suffering. His family was suffering.

After returning home from Lebanon Adrian

had been transferred to a new posting. He had time on his hands in the evenings, and it dawned on him that he was doing enough ruminating, and maybe he should get the body moving again. 'I started back walking around the area. There were beautiful lakes, canals and woods,' he recalls. 'I picked out three different routes, walked every day and created a bit of routine and structure.' On these long walks he began to notice that he was 'at war' with himself. All of the walks he took were alone. Many times he had to force himself to get out 'when it would have been easier to sit inside'. His intention was clear. 'Get into gear. Get out and maybe even time the walks.' Competition with the self can be motivating, as Adrian learned.

In developing the habit, 'the walking was shifting the focus away from my inner self and my thoughts,' he recalls. Every walk, even though sometimes boring, brought something new and different for Adrian to notice. The weather, the wind, the wildlife. He noticed a new sense of well-being. There was a sense of connectedness.

This was not the practise of learned formal meditation but the natural emergence of the mind state of just being with the world, in a different way. This can happen if we take the time to slow down. To breathe, look and listen, and let mind and body work together. We can do this even in the most challenging mental and physical circumstances. Adopting this mindful practise began to work its magic for Adrian. Each day he would go out. Each day was different. It was taking his mind off the inner anxiety. Walking is a natural medication in its own right.

Informal meditation, for Adrian, was as simple as looking out on a lake, noticing and wondering with natural curiosity. 'Instead of having negative thoughts you are inclined to have more positive ones,' he remembers.

Adrian's early solitary walks carried a sense of loneliness also. He had to really push himself. Aloneness can be a frightening state to approach, when we are used to the camaraderie and collegiality of an organisation such as the army. Notwithstanding this supportive aspect of groups, men can often cut themselves off also without feeling able to talk about the particular challenges they face. But Adrian was alone now, and he faced it.

Adrian was encouraged to join a hill-walking group of retired former colleagues. With this group it was different. While each one of the group had their own pain and potholes to describe, there was acceptance and a space to be as you are. Ten years on, this hill-walking group is still important for Adrian. But interestingly, he feels contentedly alone in this group; he describes it as 'me, myself and my shadow'. It gives him time to think, to explore his emotions.

The group walks the hills every week in a different location. There is an openness and emptiness in remote places that can heal. 'It's like crossing a barrier into a new life every time,' he says. It is a 'better way to live, be connected with my mind and body and surroundings'. On the mountain, the natural flow of life can carry us with ease.

While hill-walking is one of the most important tools in his 'toolbox', there is another. Awareness of self. That is awareness borne out of his life experience, both good and bad. Some of the deeper potholes have offered him the most learning.

Adrian's story points us to the importance of taking action, even to the extent of forcing yourself to do so. Initially this may be difficult, but it creates an impetus and a motivation which builds upon what it knows. It also builds on the core needs of every human being, that is purpose, meaning, self-efficacy ('I can') and confidence. In PTSD and depression, our levels of confidence, self-efficacy and self-esteem are poor. Through understanding himself in greater awareness, Adrian tends not to believe the movie in his head, and carries onward as best he can. There are times when that movie reels itself back, but he can halt the flood of emotions and sensations it brings. As a man, he has discovered he can let go. He can cry.

After years of actual war and inner struggle, peace is breaking out and reappearing in his life. The challenge is to rebuild. Intentional activities are central to this transformative process of recovery, and he undertook one: walking. The rebuild has taken time. There is a sense that things will be as they will be but the hope is there that they will turn out better. This is a more flexible state of mind, freely chosen. For Adrian, hill-walking provides a challenge, as well as solitude, freedom and time to reflect. It helps him to let go, to live in the moment. It lifts his mood. It energises him. He is alone, but he belongs. He now travels on in hope. We can all do this, even if we have to force ourselves. Let Adrian be an inspiration.

ASCENDING FROM DESPAIR: MOUNT KILIMANJARO

Attempting to walk to the summit of Mount Kilimanjaro can change you. For many, the thought of trekking up Kilimanjaro seems extreme and even madcap; an altogether impossible challenge. But wherever you find yourself in this moment in your life, you could probably do it with the right preparation and training, both physical and mental. Just take a moment now to go back to your diary and make a few mindful notes as to what might need to happen to get to the top of Kilimanjaro. Even if going there is totally unlikely, you might like to imagine it fantastically, as if going there virtually. Make a note of the training you would need to do and the preparation you would need to undertake to climb Kilimanjaro. What equipment do you think you might need? How fit would you need to be? What do you consider is the biggest challenge you might face? How long would you need to prepare for beforehand? Where could you go to get advice on all of this?

The chattering 'monkey mind' might be giving advice to you in the background. Take some time to reflect on what your thoughts are telling you, on what is holding you back. Make a list of those things. Is it your current uncertainty and fear of the unknown? Is it your fitness level? Your weight? In all of this, take a moment to centre yourself, by noticing your breathing as it goes in and out. Relax into your breath. Now consider mindfully the obstacles that are holding you back. Having done that, make a list of those obstacles in your diary, and consider what you might need to remove these. Also, make a list of the benefits you perceive in Kilimanjaro at this time. Don't laugh, treat this seriously. By making a list and writing it down you are in effect bringing an idea to life. You are making it more real.

In travelling to remote, high-altitude places, preparation is crucial. The walk to Kilimanjaro takes between five and nine days, and many people do it in a week. It is not especially different to other treks in terms of distance and height gained. Notwithstanding, the move through five climatic changes in as many days and the increasing demands of altitude carry with them their individual challenges. But common sense and a steady pace enable reasonable acclimatisation, challenged by inevitable moments of crisis.

Companionship leads to exchange and discovery. Friendships are the relationships we choose to nourish when we are exposed like this. On the trail everyone has a story, and friendships are formed around these stories. There is the necessary practical and emotional exchange and support within the group which helps to negotiate any crisis encountered. From all of this the pillars of confidence and resilience emerge within us. This is the wonder of taking on a challenge beyond our comfort zone and mindfully engaging with it.

Initial impressions weave together the atmosphere of an environment. This was certainly true of the ethereal lichen trees we passed on the way to Shira Plateau which lies under the summit of Kilimanjaro. They were eerily embellished with hanging moss, like something out of a Sherlock Holmes movie. But something was stirring in me with discomfort. I seemed to catch a dark mood in the landscape in those moments of unreal light and atmospheric effect. It was only a thought. We walked on.

An eight-hour walking day of constant driving rain, sleet and snow at 15,000 feet introduced a sense of unnecessary reality on the sixth day of seven before attempting the summit. I was tired, wet and cold to the marrow. My tent mate was some distance behind me on the trail, and the physical and mental demands of the days walking along and having to put up a tent alone necessitated 20 minutes of silent hypothermic rocking in the deluged privacy of my tent. My lingering despair was abruptly interrupted upon the tardy arrival of this tent mate. The pleasantries exchanged at that low moment were not altogether mindful but suffice to say that new levels of understanding were achieved in the shared challenge of the day. Honest conversation is good. Sometimes all you have to say is 'I've had a fairly bad day,' and the other person gets the picture. We are only human.

The constant cycle of natural change which for the most part passes unnoticed beside us was brought into stark relief at Lava Tower, as cloud and sun bursts, wind, rain and snow fought for supremacy. We struggled to maintain our basic comforts and prepare for the final unknown challenge of the summit. This didn't feel like holidays. Had someone suggested that we depart at 10pm on a Saturday night and walk and scramble 5,000 feet in a little under 11 hours over an oxygen-deprived, boulder-strewn, ice-packed, sub-zero landscape, I might have laughed at them, but when I noticed that my water bottle had frozen, I realised I was on holiday. Strange! I had no choice but to collect myself, and climb on.

Sometimes the severity of the challenge exacerbates the unconscious way that we are dealing with it already. I can't say that I was noticing things mindfully that day, beyond trying to make myself less uncomfortable. Like everyone else on the trek, all of my personal physical and mental resources were mobilised to deal with the challenge in a very automatic way, on autopilot. This is the nature of 'doing' and giving us the best chance of coming through a demanding ordeal. In order to survive we don't have to over-think. The benefit of this is that you tend to keep going, if sometimes unwisely.

But the sight of my frozen water bottle jolted me out of this automatic thinking, which was not preparing me very well for the challenge ahead. It allowed me to notice my emotions, refocus on the task at hand and prepare better for the 11 hours that lay ahead.

The travel writer Robert Macfarlane writes in *Mountains of the Mind* that 'when we walk or climb up a mountain, we traverse not only the actual terrain of the hillside, but also the metaphysical territories of struggle and achievement'. The human condition is laid bare on the mountain like nowhere else, in all its duality. Approach/avoid, success/failure, security/insecurity. Values, goals and actions become apparent. It is out on the rawness of that mountain that mindfulness can find its place. To breathe in and out, remember your surroundings and that your place in them is a humbling experience. Mindful walking adds value beyond any perceived goal, whether you achieve that goal or not. If you go mindfully the goal is unimportant. It is each step that is important.

What matters in a place like Kilimanjaro are not the everyday concerns of life but adventure and challenge. The walk teaches us a lot about ourselves and the importance of relationships. On any walk that challenges you mentally and physically you become aware of your strengths and weaknesses in the most raw sense. You learn to accept what is rather than wishing that things were different. You may not even get to the summit of Kilimanjaro. This acceptance is the cornerstone of resilience.

In travelling to remote places and taking on a challenge like Kilimanjaro you come to remember that most of the world is not as lucky as you. During our time in Kenya and Tanzania on our way to Kilimanjaro, the poverty was apparent. Access to medical treatments so taken for granted at home can seem like miracles to local people. On a trip like this you might even relearn your purpose in life. For a medical doctor who was a member of our group, learning that purpose was to rediscover his vocation when, on waking one morning in our campsite, he found locals gathering to be seen by him. Somehow the word had spread that he was a doctor, and an impromptu clinic had formed on the slopes of Kilimanjaro. Rather than have to write another prescription or sick note, which was what some of his patients only required of him at home, he was able to provide simple thyroid medication to a goitre sufferer, which to that person seemed like a miracle. We take so much for granted: food, clean running water from a tap, shelter, Internet access 24/7. When we aren't mindful of our riches, our impatience when things don't work out or happen quickly enough can eat away at us. A little suffering can be good on a walk to Kilimanjaro. It puts the suffering of others in perspective. We might be less impatient when we get home.

Resilient people are open to possibility and new ways. To be mindful is to be open. If you are closed then the world will pass you by. That world can also seem to fulfil the negative prophesies you have made, and confirm your worst fears and prejudices. To be mindful is to slow down, be patient, and reach out when the challenge is greatest. On the mountain this is not optional, it is a necessity.

Travelling mindfully to places such as the Camino de Santiago and Mount Kilimanjaro widens perspectives beyond the sleepy comfort zone. It extends us into the world around us. By undertaking challenges which can sometimes involve discomfort we build confidence and strength to face unforeseen misfortunes. In so doing, we can perform more effectively, develop our potential and move closer to the well-being, happiness and peace that can be so elusive.

'All the world's a stage, And all the men and women merely players; They have their exits and their entrances, And one man in his time plays many parts.' William Shakespeare, *As You Like It*

8

MINDFUL WALKING AND PERFORMANCE

In my own exploration of mindfulness I have often, like many others I'm sure, gone to lectures and presentations to listen to the wisdom of monks and practitioners from various meditation and mindfulness traditions. I have always found the opportunity to listen and learn of great benefit. It appeals to me. The wisdom and simplicity of these inspiring people is shared with the audience at these events, only for me and the audience to return to our outside world and the monks to return to their monasteries, their inner silence and meditation. I'm sure others in the audience like me would wish to have the luxury from time to time of taking ourselves away from the interference of life like those monks. But no, life and the performance go on. Most of us simply have to get up and go to work every morning.

Whether it's in an office, a hospital, a building site, a beauty salon, at home with our children or our grandchildren, or sitting writing job applications, we have a purpose to fulfil every day and this sometimes means returning to tasks we don't like having to do. As the film *Into Great Silence* showed, even the silent monks in the Grande Chartreuse monastery in France work hard to be self-sufficient – preparing food, distributing food, making their habits with the tailor. How can we incorporate what we've learned from mindful walking into working?

BACK ON THE WORLD'S STAGE

We have looked at the mindful wonder of being a spectator at a play, when our attention is hinged to the stage and the room is fused together in laughter or pathos. But we are also performers and actors in our own lives. What parts we choose to play and how we choose to play them are important to how we set about our performance. Our daily life is our performance made up of words and stories that we tell ourselves and others. The Irish playwright John B. Keane once said, 'Words have personalities.' Words have ideas wrapped up in them. The words we use are as important as how we put them into action.

Earlier in the book we discussed challenge in our lives. Three steps were mentioned in terms of how we engage with those challenges. Talk about it, meditate on it, or take some physical exercise. Throughout the book the invitation has been to explore the benefits of mindful walking in all the rich and varied forms and places described. It might help us now to take a look at the work of the well-known business coach Timothy Gallwey, who, before his time, as it were, advocated a mindful practise in our working lives. A tennis coach who used meditation to improve his game, in his 1971 book *The Inner Game of Work*, Gallwey presented a formula of four powerful words which are helpful to draw on here in summary. It really is impossible to characterise the complexity of the human condition by a formula and still, as a coaching psychologist and mindfulness practitioner, I constantly return to this one:

Performance = Potential minus Interference

Performing well in life is not about pretending, it is about being courageous, deeply true to yourself and cultivating a mindful approach to your calling. As Adrian pointed out in the story of his long walks to acceptance, a more mindful approach to life is based on awareness of self. Now let's look at how 'Potential minus Interference' can help us. As seen in previous chapters, our negative, fear-based thinking can be the source of much of the interference that prevents us from growing and developing the unique potential that we all have. We can develop very creative but ultimately unhelpful strategies to avoid challenge. If we keep doing this over a long period, we can come to believe the narrative we tell ourselves. 'I'm not able. I won't be good enough. Someone else will do it better,' or however it is you construct that narrative yourself. Coming to a greater mindful awareness of our own patterns of thinking unlocks the door to our true potential. You now have the choice to walk through that door and shine a light on that potential.

At this point, take a moment to reflect and diary. You might ask yourself the question, to what degree am I the creator of much of the interference in my life?

This reflection is also about a mindful use of the wonderful brain that we have. Our brain is not confined exclusively to our intelligence quotient (IQ) as measured by many mainstream education systems. There is our often forgotten, but equally important, emotional quotient (EQ). Having a way to regulate our emotions in demanding situations and to respond rather than to react is emotional intelligence. So far, we have heard the inspirational stories of wonderful people who have applied their learning, however painful it was, to improving their performance and making their lives more enjoyable and happier. All of the people mentioned have in many ways demonstrated the benefits of hard-learned emotional intelligence. Mindfulness is about an emotionally intelligent approach to life.

STEP UP: UNLOCK YOUR POTENTIAL TO PERFORM

Let us pause to revisit how the mind works. This is relevant because a better understanding of how the mind works gives us the evidence-based proof some of us need to incorporate and build on the benefits of a more mindful approach to our lives. It also firmly establishes mindfulness as a practise in the overall context of a full mind/body/relationships understanding of performance. This evidence arises from the field of positive psychology and is very much complementary to mindfulness and its practise.

There is much individual difference at the heart of human performance. The one shared piece of kit we all possess is the brain and thinking mind. To perform well you need to use that thinking mind to its optimum and it is not just about IQ. Earlier in this book we looked at Daniel Kahneman's Systems 1 and 2 (fast and slow) thinking, and which can be worked into our understanding of mindfulness or what we have called here System 3 thinking. Now let us take a look at how we can mindfully perform to a better future.

Human performance can be broadly understood as a continuum, from unsatisfactory to satisfactory. It is not a set point in the sense that our performance levels remain static over time. These levels can and do change, and you have a big say in that change. Your performance is a function of the following areas, as first mentioned by the psychologists Frank Gardner and Zella Moore in their book *The Psychology of Enhancing Human Performance: The Mindfulness-Acceptance Commitment Approach*, which I have adapted to fit with the mind/ body/relationships sections of this book:

- **Your physical and mental skills, abilities and competencies.** These competencies include how we move and think and act in the world. There are multiple intelligences at work here. It is not all about IQ. Maybe you are an engineer, but also an expert at directing a ball into a net.

- **External environmental and performance demands.** These include challenges that we must face in dealing with people, problems and tasks. Sometimes we might have to acknowledge that we have been thrown off balance by these challenges or in some instances it might appear like we have been thrown by the wayside. When we have lost our job it might feel like we have fallen off the cliff. How we deal with these challenges boils down to whether we get the balance of our mindful thinking and non-thinking right or not. Do we respond or react?

- **Internal dispositional characteristics.** These internal elements include our personality type (introvert / extrovert), our coping style (approach / avoid), and our explanatory style (optimist / pessimist). These elements go to make up the way we perceive, interpret and respond to particular performance stimuli and demands before us. Here are some questions for you to ask yourself, and perhaps jot down the answers to. How would you describe your personality? What is your coping style? How do you explain your world? How do you perform under stress? How do you relax? How would you describe your attitude overall?

- **Emotional intelligence and fitness.**
  These include managing and regulating
  the thinking, emotions and behaviours
  that are likely to give us the best
  chance of good performance. On his
  blog, well-known coach Anthony
  Robbins talks about three fundamental
  traits that create the capacity to lead.
  These can also be applied to emotional
  fitness. We can: a) See things as they
  are, not worse that they are; b) See
  things better than they are; and c)
  Make things the way we see them.

  We have a tendency to predict
  the future negatively, which only
  adds to the pain we are experiencing.
  We need to move away from this
  way of thinking. Even in negative
  circumstances there is always
  possibility. With mindfulness, you may
  deliberately focus your attention on
  the positive, thereby allowing for the
  possibility to move on from a negative
  or harmful emotional situation.

An important point needs to be nailed here before
moving on. Our performance is a physical and

mental process. Mindful walking is about our physical and mental well-being. Imagine a line with a break-even point marked in the middle at zero (0), a lowest score of -100 marked on the line to the far left and a highest score of +100 marked on the line 'Beyond Zero' to the far right. It might help to draw out the line on a blank sheet. Where do you currently rate your performance? Is it in minus or plus figures? Whether you rate yourself as above or below the zero (0), you are rating your mental health.

Mental health is about our performance. It varies in response to life generally. With catastrophic, life-changing events, our performance can dip well below the break-even point. Any figure mentioned on this continuum is only a starting point to better performance. A lower performance figure should not be stigmatised. It should be understood. With appropriate therapy, counselling or coaching we can all move back to a better place.

Moving back to a better place involves a clear understanding of what is likely to work best for us. In meeting the challenges we face, do we focus our attention on the task at hand, or do we focus on ourselves?

This is the choice between, on the one hand,

having the best chance of dealing with the situation, and on the other, remaining stuck. The important thing here is to notice things beyond the self and inflexible demands in terms of the negative thinking, beliefs and rules that we apply to ourselves. (When we tell ourselves things like 'I must', 'I should', 'I have to' or 'I am inadequate', 'I will fail'.)

The evidence relating to human performance highlights that people who perform well focus on task-relevant cues rather than task-irrelevant cues, such as self-doubt, inadequacies, and overly exaggerated self-criticism about performance failures. We must remind ourselves to enjoy the process, as well as seek the outcome. Focus on the task, with a gentle eye on the self. Life can be like walking mindfully. It can be liberating, free and beautiful. If, when we walk mindfully, we continue thinking about ourselves, telling ourselves we are falling off the cliff, then most assuredly, we have a greater chance of doing just that.

When you learn to focus your attention on the broad picture in a less judgemental, more mindful way, you begin to loosen up and adopt a lightness of step, an openness to life, beyond fear-based performance. It is energising and empowering and gives you a freedom to be and act naturally.

You are who you are. You can become a first-rate version of yourself. That potential can be unleashed. Mindfully walking into your future can be a fundamental part of this process.

With this freedom, you have a choice to experiment in a different way. Adopting the practise of mindfulness and mindful walking can release the power of the conceptual mind, beyond fear. Mindfulness and mindful walking engages the body in this process. As a consequence of our practise, we don't fall into the pothole and find ourselves trapped in the conceptual grasping mind which is fearfully attached to outcomes. Make a list, create a vision, learn from your mistakes, but all the while maintain the focus on the present moment where the best decisions and responses can be made in greater freedom. Far from speeding up, we need to create more space to slow down from time to time and just observe our own style. Watch our pattern of thinking, feeling and behaving, and accept it.

> 'I would love to live
> Like a river flows,
> Carried by the surprise
> Of its own unfolding.'
> John O'Donohue

My Mindful Future

Set aside this book and take a few moments. If it is convenient, wherever you find yourself and in whatever posture is comfortable, recall your intention to focus on your breathing. Try a meditation for the next 10 minutes. Set a timer for yourself. Remember there is no goal in this meditative exercise. Begin it with an attitude of curiosity and openness.

1. Start by bringing your attention to the natural ebb and flow of your breath. Allow your mind to settle. If you need to adjust your posture, do so gently. This is quite normal. The object is not to remain absolutely still. It is to develop awareness and calmness of both body and mind.

2. By simply focusing on the breath, the inhalation and the exhalation, you can bring a deep calmness to your body. Reuniting with your breath allows any held tension in the body to be released.

3. Observing the breath can teach us many things. Because of our inherited disposition,

the conditioning and habituation from our earliest years, our unconscious and conscious mind can go out of control from time to time. The paradox of mindfulness, non-thinking and non-striving, the very process of non-judgemental observation of our judgemental thoughts, can bring a calm yet alertness which the conceptual mind may be in need of. In practising mindfulness and mindful walking we can come to know the step of our own style. A brighter future can emerge from this place of calmness and awareness, which is the foundation of well-being, happiness and ultimately peace.

4. When you have completed your mindful meditation, bring yourself back to your diary and take another few moments to reflect on what you have noticed. Try to capture your mood and energy levels. What is your motivation now? What are you noticing that might be relevant as you move forward with your life and work? How confident are you now in doing that?

In moving forward now to unlock your potential to maximise your performance, getting the balance of your thinking right is critical. This is a balance between the processing power of the brain, either conscious or unconscious, and the power of mindfulness as you become the observer of that thinking. When Systems 1 and 2 and System 3 are aligned you are more likely to achieve the results you were asked to imagine at the beginning of this book. These results include, for most people, controlling your emotions, making better decisions, improving your memory and creativity, reducing stress. Not only have you a way of maximising the power of the thinking brain but you have a way of controlling its wandering activity by simply observing it non-judgementally. The doing and the being are in equilibrium. Mind and body are aligned.

Thinking and Non-Thinking: FORM and FARM

We can make this distinction even clearer

by using the following acronyms: FORM and FARM. Acronyms are supercharged words with powerful personalities. And they're easy to remember. I have always found this method of thinking very helpful.

FORM the inner landscape of the mind to FARM the outer landscape of your world. In FORMing the inner landscape, you tune into and become aware of their own style of thinking. This is mindfulness. All of the postures described so far, such as sitting meditation, body scan and mindful standing and walking, embrace this approach. In learning to train the mind you are by extension asked to act in a different way that may serve you more effectively. By changing the way you view things, you may also change the way you do things. FARMing the external landscape of your life, you can become more mindful in the process. This opportunity to FORM the inner landscape is a lifestyle choice that has implications for your well-being, happiness, peace and contentment. Let's break down these acronyms into some more detail.

FORM the Present: 'Don't just do something, sit there'

- **Focus** on your unfolding experience in a non-judgemental way. Pay attention mindfully. Notice your thoughts, feelings and sensations in the body wherever they arise. Can you notice them, even when the experience might be negative? 'It is flogging down with rain outside as I write', you might think. 'This is Ireland but I know it will pass and how lucky am I to be inside in relative comfort,' you might then remind yourself.

- **Observe** in a mindful way. You are the master by simply observing the happenings around you. No need to judge. No need to become attached to these happenings. No need to act in this moment.

- **Review** and reflect in curiosity on your overall awareness of thoughts, emotions and sensations in the body.

This is not necessarily a part of formal mindfulness practise, but reflection is the basis of new awareness and learning. Maybe capture this as well in your diary.

- Make new **meaning** for yourself and begin finding out the way you want to live your life. This will emerge naturally in the overall process of mindfully FORMing the present in a more optimistic way.

FARM the Future: 'Don't just sit there, do something'

- **Focus** on all your experience in a non-judgemental way.

- **Act** and experiment on new tasks that will build on your learning and experience. How could you begin to join the dots of that experience in new ways? Take up something new that you have always wanted to do. Prepare to fail at it, prepare to enjoy it. Make a list to articulate the intention and conviction towards your new task. Keep making lists as they are mindful provocations to action.

- **Review** and reflect on the beliefs and rules you are currently applying to how you live your life. Are they serving you well? Using the brain is energy sapping. Don't forget to rest.

- Make new **meaning** for yourself and the way you want to live your life.

FORM the present to FARM the future.

The FORM and FARM methods both embrace the core elements of a mindful, focused approach to life. Observing, noticing and bringing attention to perceptions, assumptions, rules, beliefs, feelings and sensations, wherever they arise in mind and body, is how we do this. The starting point can simply be a mindful walk. We develop a mindful walking practise where we remain present with our current experience, even when it is unpleasant or downright painful. We develop a mindful walking practise where we adopt a non-judgemental stance in respect of all of our experience. We don't resist. We don't struggle. We don't tell ourselves that we shouldn't be feeling the way we are feeling. On this mindful walk we are learning, we can go at our own pace: step back, think, observe, proceed, STOP from time to time and as necessary, FORM and FARM.

In adopting this way of being with our experience we can learn to name and know the beliefs, assumptions and needs that may not be serving us well. We can review and reflect on what they are, and ask ourselves how they fit into our lives. This way of being with our experience is the precursor to new ways of viewing and new ways of doing in our lives. In all of this we can develop positive strategies and appropriate responses to our internal experience, thinking and feeling. We can respond rather than react. Non-reaction can be practised. In all of this we are thinking and feeling and behaving in greater awareness. We are not sleepwalking or numb or dead before we die. We are tuning the mind. We are alive to whatever arrives and have a better chance of dealing with it in an emotionally intelligent manner.

The Immutable Truth of CRAIC

There are two immutable truths about you and your performance. Let's acknowledge them;

- In anything that you do, you can perform better than you currently think or feel. You can have more fun and enjoyment and it is not all about pleasure. The Irish word 'craic', pronounced 'crack', points the way. The concept of craic, and its play on words that evokes the dangerous chemical drug, without any of its consequences, might help us to see where the real fun is. Craic involves understanding what you can **Control**, taking full **Responsibility** for yourself, developing a greater sense of **Awareness**, developing an **Impetus** and motivation to move beyond your comfort zone, and ultimately, developing a greater mindful **Confidence** in your own ability to be the captain of your ship.

- In mindfully walking on, your increasing awareness is giving you greater choice. Change is happening right now. You can move forward. A good friend of mine once told me, 'You shouldn't be at it if you are not enjoying yourself.' The challenge now is to incorporate more mindful CRAIC into your life.

THE WORDS TO TAKE WITH US

There are three final value-laden words we might reflect on now. They underscore a mindful engagement with your performance and how you wish to play your part on the world's stage. The psychologist and mindfulness teacher Shauna Shapiro mentions these three words as being central to the practise of mindfulness: Intention, Attention and Attitude. They are no less central to the practise of mindful walking.

Intention

Intentionality is a skill we need to develop. It

creates possibility. It drives change. Mindful intentions drive our thinking and our language. Actions follow. Our behaviour is then congruent with our actions. Stating an intention does not necessarily get us to our destination. It does however create the best conditions to get there. Aligning our intentions with our goals in a flexible and adaptable way builds on those favourable conditions.

Unexpected events could happen en route to any destination but a clear statement of intent and associated preparation generates energy and a motivation which moves mind and body to take on the challenge and the uncertainty. Movement is good.

Taking the first steps creates energy and a tangible impetus of its own. If we are mindful we can even see this intention in the way we walk. The first steps are built around words of intent. These positive words of intent and our commitment are in effect creating the future.

Effecting the change we want to see in ourselves involves great and trusting intentionality. In our performance, intentionality is about reassessing what is important to us. It is fundamentally about what now drives you on your journey forward, wherever you choose to go. It is not really about the destination or the summit. That will come soon enough. For Adrian, it was to drag himself out to walk when he least wanted to. For Tim it was to accept that it was ok to let go. For Sarah it was to embrace a new outlet of mind/body exercise, when walking wasn't possible. For Johnny Barnes it was the intention to show up every morning. In the context of performance, intentionality is the starting point for every new experience. It sets the direction in which we wish to take our lives in a more meaningful way. Intentionality should be aligned with what nourishes us as human beings. In setting clear intentions, there is no blind conviction that matters will unfold as we might wish. Life is not like that. In aligning our practise of mindfulness with our intentions, mindful doing follows. Our performance becomes more effective and we are more likely to keep ourselves in contention and get to that summit.

In doing what you do, what is your intention? Know this. It might be to move job. It might be to start that course you have been promising yourself. It might be just to do something tomorrow that you have never done before, such as walk 500 metres on a new street or pathway. It might be to go to Toastmasters through your workplace, and face your fear of public speaking. Whatever that intention is, align it with the person you are or who you wish to become. Align your intentions with your values to give added meaning. In aligning your intentions in a flexible and adaptable way with your values, goals and actions, you are being true to yourself but also allowing yourself room to fail and learn. Being different, taking risks and failing is good. This is what makes us. Only you know what that looks like. Take responsibility now. It is your unique story. Write it now, even on a single blank page of your diary, based on your intentions for the future.

Write down what it is you want to achieve. Describe it in detail. Write down why you want to achieve it, how it is going to be measured and when you are going to have it completed by. In all of this it will help that whatever you set out to do is realistic within the time frame set. In all of this, bear in mind that setting big, hairy, audacious intentions would be like eating an elephant, difficult to swallow all in one go. Be prepared to break down the challenge into manageable pieces. Like walking mindfully as this book suggests, for ten minutes a day. It is amazing what you can get through step by step by breaking down the task and focusing on the here and now.

Attention

Mindfulness is about developing the skill to focus our attention. In breathing deeply, we are taking the opportunity to inspire ourselves to just be in the moment. In this simple act we are FORMing the future, in the now. Mindfully focusing on our unfolding experience, we observe it non-judgementally in a reflective manner and make necessary new meaning.

In adopting a mindful FORM and FARM approach to our life we are both the actor / performer and the spectator, 'doing' and 'being' naturally and in a more balanced way. We can relate to our thinking so that we are more present to the challenge and the requirements of that challenge, whatever emerges, good or bad. It will inevitably not turn out exactly the way you planned it. Mindfulness and mindful walking are about being flexible and adaptable.

In walking mindfully through life we can be both an effective performer and observer in the play. In developing the mindful practise of focusing our attention non-judgementally we won't get lost in negative thoughts or let our minds wander to the same degree, because then we are neither an effective actor / performer or an observer.

At any time of the day we can make it our intention to take time to focus mindfully and make new meaning for ourselves. We can make it an intention and decide on an ongoing basis what is most effective for our overall performance. We give ourselves a chance to review whether our current thinking is effective and what is best required for this present moment. We can change in spite of the understandable and ever-present interference.

It is amazing when you think that what you attend to and focus on gets done! Focus on the challenge. On the walk of life that might simply be the next mindful step. What you practise gets better! Keep doing it. Keep moving. Persist. Persevere. You will almost certainly surprise yourself if you keep doing the simple things well. Mindfulness is about developing the skill to focus your attention where it is likely to be most effective.

Now this very moment, where are you and what are you noticing? Ask yourself this. Tomorrow, ask yourself this again. And next week, ask yourself once more. Write down your answers, and reflect on them. Mindfulness advances our understanding of our own mind, how it works, the thinking patterns evident and the emotions and behaviours associated. To develop the muscle of mindfulness, focus is the key, and practise is the oil to unlock inner potential, strength and confidence.

Ultimately, happiness, well-being and peace emerge not in their own right but as a by-product of our intentions and this mindful meaning-making process. Happiness emerges, not as an entitlement or a requirement of the walk of life but as part of a full, present-moment, mindful participation in that walk, which can be challenging, demanding and even painful at times.

Attitude

'Everything can be taken from a man but one thing: the last of human freedoms – to choose one's attitude in any given set of circumstances, to choose one's own way.' Viktor Frankl

If there is one element of the human condition that impacts to the most profound degree on our performance in life and work, then it must be attitude. Our attitude is about our beliefs, moods, feelings and the manner in which we verbally or non-verbally act out on the world around us, or choose not to. That world is made up of people and groups and all of the symbols and rituals associated. If we find ourselves built into a particular attitude, we might adopt a tendency to judge our experience as good or bad, favourable or unfavourable. And we might misjudge what we find.

No matter how well-educated we are, how

much money we have, how good looking we feel, how gifted or skilled we may be, it is our attitude that will ultimately make or break us as compassionate humans, and the relationships we have with others which support us along the way.

The underlying power of mindfulness is that in choosing to practise it in all its postures and contexts – on city streets, on the mountain, in the garden or the city parks – we can become aware of a profound truth. That is that we are the only ones who can choose the attitude we adopt in any given situation. If that attitude is based on arrogance or insecurity, attachment or fear, then the toxic results will become apparent all too quickly.

How about looking at ourselves through a new reality? Reminding ourselves that the past cannot be changed. Telling ourselves that it was what it was. The future cannot be predicted, and people will behave in the way they behave. The only personal power left with us is the attitude we choose to adopt in any given situation. Do we emotionally hijack and react impulsively, or do we develop a mindful attitude, through which we can always choose a more appropriate response?

This is the choice that the practise of mindfulness offers. This is the overarching 'meta' or 'self' perspective that mindful walking gives us when we realise our place in life. We are all here to make a difference in our own unique way.

What legacy do we wish to leave to our family and those we work with? Is it the legacy of the bully or the angry man, or is it something more worthwhile?

The Winter Solstice

The twin peaks of the 'Paps' or 'Breasts of Anu' dominate the ancient derelict city of Shrone which lies to the north-east of the Cork/Kerry border in the south-west of Ireland. Its walls enclose rich archaeological artefacts that connect us not only with history but with a symbolic significance. The wider area is known as Sliabh Luachra, meaning fertile or shining hill. It has a long and rich tradition of poetry and music.

It is a much-visited area and at this time of year has even more significance, as many climb to the top to await the sunrise on the winter solstice. On this the longest night and the shortest day of the year in the northern hemisphere, the earth's axis is tilted 23.5 degrees away from the sun. There is very little light to guide the way.

I am there with a group of companions to mark this special date in the winter calendar. From this morning on, the days will get longer, brightness will overcome darkness. It is a hopeful time of year.

The early pace of this morning is somewhat hectic in a purposeful way, the walkers all wearing their headlamps and talking with a nervous excitement. I decide not to wear mine, as it appears that the lights and speed of the city still illuminate our group. There is a peak to be climbed. There are two of them in fact and all before sunrise. Wasn't that the intention?

'One step at a time,' I say to myself as I walk to the rear of the chattering group. The headlamps in front keep flashing and distracting me as height is gained. 'No good,' I mumble silently and in frustration. 'I can't accurately judge my footfall. I have no sense of depth.' I am beginning to be disoriented.

Headlamps are powerful in the pitch of any winter's morning at 6am. In the back shadows of my companions' reflected and constantly shifting headlamps I feel like I am coming apart mentally and physically. It is a strange feeling. I struggle to keep up. I have a decision to make.

Sometimes you need to keep moving. Sometimes you need to stop. Do I stop, quickly put on my own headlamp and mindlessly plough on? Do I stay part of the group? I make my choice. In this instance I slow down. My shadow catches up.

Shortly I am in the Scary Place between light and dark, between aloneness and belonging. I watch the lights of the group merge into one. Soon they are gone.

And then alone, the squawking egoic mind starts. Thoughts fill the silence: 'You should have stayed with the group. They've gone on!' 'You have no light.' 'Not so bright now, is it?' 'Will they be ok?' 'Will I be ok?'

Standing there, the body is confused too. There

was some comfort, if painful, in the blinding light. Although inadequate and disorienting, the light was in some strange way real and familiar. I move on at my own pace and under my own terms. It's ok to do that too. 'Slow down. Breathe deeply. One step at a time. Stop. Rest. Look around.' I make a conscious effort to appreciate the progress made. 'I am still heading in the right direction. I am grateful for that.'

In these moments I feel deeply connected with a wider, striving humanity. The challenge of trusting the process was still being frequently undermined by my chattering mind. But mindfully focusing on one breath at a time, one step at a time, brings me back to the present moment and the task at hand.

The challenge on those twin peaks that day was to be fully present to the experience, so that I could accept the uncertainty, anxieties and frustrations in a gentler, more compassionate way that didn't drain my energy and reduce my effectiveness. It was difficult, but I had been in similar situations before. Experience and learning just do not appear like magic; they accumulate like a harvest. You start at the start and you build from there.

Inherent in the human condition is a polarity of mind and body states. Light and dark. Comfort and discomfort. Success and failure. Right and wrong. Happiness and sadness. We have complex and competing 'mind states' within us all. There are no simple answers to building the muscle of mindful experience. In working with these competing mind states in a mindful way we can achieve balance even in demanding and challenging situations such as walking a mountain on a winter solstice at night. We can mindfully build our experience, step by step, on the journey, on the walk. Even in the darkest places we can do that. In such places we can train ourselves to quiet the mind in the midst of fear, uncertainty and anxiousness. In taking on the challenge we can learn a better way.

'I can't stay where I am.' For some reason the thought of going back comes to mind again. I move on, each step uncertain and laboured. I slip. I fall to one knee. Fortunately, there is no rock to land on this time. Luck is part of the walk too. It helps.

And then in slowing down, I begin to notice something different. Strangely, as my eyes acclimatise themselves to the background light, I begin to get a measure of the underfoot conditions. My night vision is improving. I am adapting.

If given a chance, the body is well equipped to be guided by the available light. In reality my body has caught up with my mind. On the mountain they are now partners in an easier, more compassionate relationship with the internal and external challenge. Life can be like that too.

By now I have found my pace and my place. Calmer now, moving one step at a time, I move on, seeing the first crest against the increasing eastern light. It is good to be home, I say to myself. Mind and body are working well together now. They are connected in a way which taps the natural inner strength and potential available to us all. I am beginning to feel good and I notice this. Confidence returns.

There is a sense of achievement in overcoming the confusion, uncertainty and fear which sometimes only the natural world and in particular a mountain at night can share with you. Great learning about the self is to be gained in that place of tension, between the inner and outer worlds of human experience.

Acting on the challenges the world presents is to face our fears. It is an experiment which builds the inner core of strength and character that is a necessary part of building confidence and resilience. This is a choice. On the mountain that morning, I understood and dealt with the challenge and interference as effectively as possible. I didn't panic this time. The egoic guardsman knew his place.

As the early morning unfolded on the mountain, my intention was clear. My attention was mindfully focused on the challenge, here and now. My attitude was positive. I let the wisdom of mind and body working together be the guide. Eventually I reconnected with my companions and we continued the journey together.

When intention, attention and attitude are aligned in a mindful, positive, compassionate way, we come alive to our potential. We build confidence. We are more resilient in the face of setback. We remain in contention.

Don't try this at home! Walking alone on an open mountain at night in the middle of winter is not something you would sensibly do, even with considerable experience in mountain craft. That is true. But also it is true that the only way that you are going to get the experience is to go to the mountain that challenges you.

In the challenge the human condition is laid bare. This is never more so than in the dark of night. There is a physical and mental challenge. It is also a time when mind and body can work in a mindfully intelligent way to meet this challenge. The seven attitudinal pillars of mindfulness (Non-Judging, Patience, Beginner's Mind, Trust, Non-Striving, Acceptance and Letting Go) begin to make sense on the mountain. They can be practised in nature, while walking gently and slowly. You can begin to see with new eyes that are more curious, less judgemental, more patient, more trusting and accepting of the world around and your place in it. You can let go and just be, while at the same time keeping a mindful eye on the path ahead. You are both the performer and the observer in your own destiny.

THE PERFORMER

Dignified, step after slow step, she mindfully walks onto the stage, noticing the surroundings and the audience. She moves with great poise. She comes to her chair and takes time to sit mindfully, and settle her cello and bow. The performance begins.

Some say that youth is wasted on the young. Not so for Sinead, a cellist with a prodigious talent. She lives her 20 years with care. There is a sense that she has time. She is not hurried. She realises how lucky she is. She exudes optimism and energy. She has her dreams. She has her goals and she is applying herself with mindful, positive intent and focus to achieve them. She is motivated to be the best she can.

She knows well that her music is a physical and mental, mind/body process, but even in the solitariness of her practise, she appreciates the importance of relationships. Challenges will come for sure but she has understood, at this very early stage in her life and career, a mindfully intelligent approach to her work and the need for balance. For someone so young, Sinead seems to mix the water and oil of youth and wisdom. It is the alchemy of youthful energy, exuberance and curiosity which can flow anywhere, mixed with the oil of wisdom which can prevent rusting.

As a performing artist, she needs to practise and master the skills of her trade. But performance is not just about knowledge, skill and competence. It is more. As a performer you put yourself out there before the public for scrutiny and judgement and possible rejection. It is a tougher world than most of us will experience.

She is fortunate. She has been exposed to a deeper learning and reflection beyond the formal education system. At an early stage of life she has been exposed to mindfulness and its practise as she learns her art. Mindfulness practise is important to Sinead because it impacts on her well-being and mental health as a full-time performer. She is living life to the full as she travels her world.

While relatively new to the practise of mindfulness, her insights are important because we are all performing artists on our own stage, with our own unique potential, fighting our own interferences. One should never be afraid to learn. Sinead is not. And we should never be afraid to learn from someone so young.

The young can teach us much but we need also to share the learning of mindfulness from an early age with our young people, our children. Training in mindfulness, both formal and informal, needs to be creatively integrated and embedded in our education system in order to maximise the potential of the next generation beyond simply academic ability. In an increasingly challenging world, emotional intelligence and fitness is a priority too for generations to come.

Let's now explore what Sinead has to share with us about mindfulness and its importance to her as an artist and performer. I interviewed her from her campus in the US where she is currently studying. Her own words in reply speak for themselves.

Interview with the Performer

Q1. Sinead, what is your understanding of mindfulness? In your own words, capture it as best you can.

A. In my eyes, mindfulness is learning how to be fully present, in each passing moment. It's about becoming more aware of your senses; and accepting the way things are, non-judgementally. It's about letting go of the past, and not dwelling too much on what the future may hold; constantly bringing yourself back to this moment, this breath.

Q2. Which qualities of mindfulness are important to you as an artist?

A. As a performing artist, we spend hours upon hours in a practise room 'perfecting' our acts, trying to plan exactly how our performance should go. It is so easy to get completely caught up about how things 'should' sound on the day, rather than how they actually do. The joy of performance is that you never really know how it will go. Every concert is different: the location, acoustics, audience, your colleagues. One of the most important qualities of mindfulness to me as an artist is learning how to accept the way things are non-judgementally. It has become clear to me over the years that a performance is never going to go the way you 'planned' – but that is not necessarily a bad thing. Performance is the art of creation – it goes where it goes! Being fully present on stage means that I can be fully open to whatever may inspire me in that moment.

Q3. What difference has the practise of mindfulness made to your performance as an artist?

A. Mindfulness has helped me not only psychologically, but physically. Being more aware of my body has been a huge factor. I have struggled with back pain and tension over the past few years, and it's only in recent weeks that I realise I am often not even aware of the tension I may be holding. Concentrating on my breathing in performances has been hugely beneficial in helping both my muscles and my mind to relax, while constantly reminding me to live in this moment.

Q4. Can you describe this difference in terms of:

a. How you think about your performance?

A. More and more I realise that technique is not what constrains us, fear is. Each time we walk out on stage, we run the risk of completely and utterly mortifying ourselves in public, in front of our friends and colleagues. In a performance, the minute it starts becoming about you ('What do they think of me right now?') you have lost the battle. It has to be about the art.

b. How you feel about your performance?

A. Whenever I walk on stage, I try to remind myself of a wonderful metaphor my professor told me. I imagine myself as three years old in playschool painting a beautiful picture for my parents. I paint our house, with the trees and the flowers and family standing outside. And I run home – full of excitement to share this with them! Of course, in reality, all that was on the page were blobs of dripping paint. But to me, I wasn't afraid of what my parents were going to think of me, all I cared about was the art! So each time I walk on stage, I say to myself: 'I made this for you.'

c.   How you actually perform in public?

A.   Mindfulness has taught me to accept the fact that not everything will go to plan, and that is hugely liberating. I am more relaxed on stage and, being fully present, I have the freedom to do things differently every time. I don't get caught up in what 'mistakes' may have happened in the last bar, because I am onto the next moment! I also find myself being more efficient in the practise room, as I try to constantly bring myself back to the present moment.

Q5. What has mindfulness taught you as a performing artist?

A.   Since I began studying in the United States a year ago, I have been hugely impressed by the emphasis that is put on the psychological side of performing, rather than simply the physical side. My teachers are constantly reminding me that 'Technique is not what constrains us, fear is.' When approaching a difficult passage in music, we are taught to think positively, for example instead of 'don't mess up, don't mess up!' or 'I hate this shift!' we are encouraged to say, 'Wow … this interval is pretty beautiful!'

We are taught to 'let go' of things which don't go our way on stage, and amazingly, we are reminded that it is ok to make mistakes! My professor once told us that he would much rather we went out on stage, took many risks and completely messed up everything, so that afterwards we could sit down and figure out what went wrong, learn from it and move on.

I was absolutely delighted to receive an email from my advisor a few weeks ago informing me that the school would now be offering 'Mindfulness Meditation' classes with a local psychologist for all performing arts students every Monday afternoon. I have been attending these classes weekly, and it has had a huge effect on me. These past few weeks have been particularly hectic, with concerts in the US and in Europe; however, mindfulness is really helping me to become much more aware of my senses. It has had both a calming and regenerating effect on me, and my 'daily routine' such as eating breakfast, walking to school, taking out my cello has become much more exciting! I am suddenly so much more conscious of all of my senses; even just holding my cello is a whole new experience. I realise I was never truly aware of the smell of the varnish, the texture of the wood and the metal strings, the incredible detail of the woodwork, the feel of the vibrations as I play. Not to mention all of the nuances in every sound that is created!

Mindfulness has taught me to experience every second of my life more fully. I feel calmer and more aware of what is going on inside and outside my body, and I am sure that I will continue to benefit from this hugely, both under the limelight and behind the scenes!

Sinead speaks very clearly about bridging and blending a way of 'doing' and 'being.' They are not separate. They are inextricably linked in her unfolding experience.

Like Sinead, for us mindfulness is about our unique psychology, how our own mind works. It works like no other, so maybe we should get to know it. This mindful knowing can have profound effects in the long term. No magic. No miracles. It is just a willingness to be present to the zest and the energy that is waiting to be unleashed.

GOT AN ATTITUDE?

A mindful approach to life is about intention, focused attention and attitude. We might have many strings to our bow; however, the one string that is the foundation of health, well-being and happiness is our attitude.

In awareness, moment by moment, we have choice regarding the attitude we will take. This choice is not something that just happens. We have to practise this attitudinal approach. This approach cannot change our inherited biological genetic make-up. However, it can change our personal psychology and how our mind works. It can change our beliefs about ourselves and others. It can begin to break some of the belief-based rules that currently don't serve us well. A favourite one is 'I would never be able to do that. I'm not going to try it.' We can break that attitude.

On the mountain or on the stage, where fear in all its forms lurks, a new sense of meaning can emerge. This pushes us further along the journey to well-being, happiness and peace. Paying attention mindfully works on us in spite of our fear.

Solving problems and doing stuff gives meaning to our lives. Meaning is found on the journey, on the walk, but we must perform to our unique strengths. We must be active actors in our lives to achieve our potential. Action and accomplishment are what give meaning to our lives. So are rest and reflection. It is a great feeling to get to the summit, but you always have to come down. There are other summits to your better world. They may not even be that high.

In all of this doing we at times get lost or stuck. Even on the walk, with all of its beneficial possibilities for mind and body and relationships, some people are still running away. At times we don't take time to slow down and stop and focus in a different way than we are used to.

The attitude you bring to a mindfully intelligent way of engaging with our unfolding experience gives you the best chance when going through heaven or hell. When going through extremes, you know that neither last indefinitely. There is an end to everything. And you have got to keep going as best you can.

This unpredictable world can be destructive not only of individuals, but also families, groups and relationships. From a psychologically-minded perspective we can understand the benefits of having some predictability and certainty in our lives. This is the need for some order and control writ large. However, much of the richness of life and learning and sharing gets lost at either end of a rigid, inflexible need for that certainty and control. How often do we see this in parents and managers and political leaders? Whether as a parent or a manager or a political leader, your future performance depends on your attitude and ability to hold uncertainty in more effective, flexible and adaptable ways. This is the place where maybe, for the first time, you have the confidence to think as best you can for yourself beyond the inner mental interference or any external dogma-based interference. In effect you are willing to plumb the depths of your potential to become what you were meant to be: just you, made from a unique mould, like nobody else.

Today, we can go mindfully beyond the fantasy, fiction and distortion of the mind. This very day, we can be at ease with ourselves, without needing anything. Be curious, appreciative, and even grateful. Things could always be better but you can only start from where you are.

In engaging with the world more mindfully, not only will we enjoy the walk of life in our aloneness, but also contribute in more positive ways to the group and our community as we go.

What would it take for you to start a Mindful Walking Group in your local area or workplace? Just put the word out there and see what happens. Invite some of your friends and colleagues to join you.

Joining a local walking group might be a good way to start also. There are many such groups dotted around the country with graded walks to

8

PARTING WORDS

Western psychology gives us insights into the complex and interrelated workings of mind and body in a social world. There is value in understanding our own style, temperament and traits as we negotiate this social world in life and work. Many of these traits are inherited but much of the way we uniquely engage with our world is learned from our earliest days. As children we learn such ways of engaging that either facilitate or inhibit the way we make sense of our world. In many ways we are all psychologists, in that for better or worse we all attempt to make sense of the world we live and work in.

We are tapping into a shared inheritance to try to rediscover an older wisdom which is increasingly seen to be complementary to modern psychology. That is the age-old practise of meditation and mindfulness. Neuroscience is also beginning to reveal the inner workings of the mind / body interactions and confirm the evidence-based value of mindfulness practise.

This book has attempted to informally integrate the insights of psychology, positive psychology in particular, with the practise of mindful walking. Mind and body come together in that social world of relationships. Therein lies the value of mindful walking.

There is an important and obvious question which has not been explicitly asked to this point. Can you pause in whatever you are doing and ask yourself the following question:

Am I flourishing? Am I truly happy, contented and at peace in my life and work at this time? Do I feel good about my life right now? Answer 'yes' or 'no.' Then ask yourself the same question at the same time tomorrow. And the next day, and the next, for the next week. Write down your answers, record them, and reflect on what they say about your current state of play.

If the answer is 'no' for too many days, then ask the following question: what is preventing me from flourishing? Go to your diary one more time and make a list of the obstacles.

Having made that list, answer the final question: what is it I might need to let go of? Mindfulness and mindful walking are about bringing us to a place where we can really see what it is that we might need to let go of.

At the beginning of this book you were asked to imagine a better way to live. In travelling some of the journey, hopefully you now have a firmer understanding of the forces that shape our performance at all levels, mind, body and relationships. These are the forces that shape our well-being, happiness and peace also. More importantly, I hope that this knowledge and practise can help you to imagine your better way.

Modern life presents inexhaustible challenges to living mindfully. It is hard to keep up with the apparent change. There is a lot of frantic doing. In the meantime, if we don't develop and master the capacity to switch off, close down and do nothing, we run the risk of worsening the already worrying consequences of this unbridled 'doing.' Our minds were not designed to think fast and slow, 7 days a week, 24 hours a day, indefinitely. There is a better way. It is the way of a more mindful walk through life and work and the enjoyment of both.

In these pages I have offered frameworks from which to observe and know and understand the self. There is a lot of advice out there urging us to be mindful but ultimately, the choice is yours. The challenge is to return from time to time to a way of being which our ancestors may have understood. That is, to slow down and walk mindfully from place to place.

The lessons of mindfulness, and mindful walking, have been known to us for thousands of years, even if they lay dormant, or far flung in the East, for some of those years. The parting gesture of this book is to ask you to take these lessons from the past and incorporate them into a new meaning and way of 'doing' and 'being.' If we don't we may consign ourselves to keep mindlessly doing what we currently are doing and getting the same negative results. Only you can decide to experiment for different results.

Walking mindfully into the future is about taking time, noticing what is important and making new meaning that will serve us and others well. This is an urgent calling, and we are only too aware of how badly it can go wrong. There is a need to develop a new awareness of ourselves and our place in the world. The implications of not doing this could be fatal.

Something we learn when we walk mindfully is that we are all connected. We are one; despite individual and group differences such as race, religion, nationality, ethnicity, we are intimately connected to each other and all that surrounds us in the wider world. What unites us is greater than what separates us. We need to nurture and share what we can for the benefit of future generations.

How the mind perceives the world can create illusion and delusion for us all. Our attempts to defend ourselves are based on the illusion of separateness and certainty. When we understand what is holding us back and discover the power of letting go, we can flow with ease like water to its ultimate conclusion. Therein lies peace, happiness and well-being.

To live mindfully is to look at the obstacles we meet along the way like passing clouds; to use the phrase of Anthony de Mello, 'Clouds come and go: some of them are black and some white, some of them are large, others small.' Those perceived obstacles can also be stepping stones to a better future. Sure the temperatures of life will rise or plummet. But inevitably we can regain the essence of our doing and being and move on. This is the power of mindfulness in a world of distraction and speed. Mindfulness and mindful walking give us all the power to quieten our minds in the midst of the chaos that is out there. A mindful walk gives us the power to reconnect to the world that bred us. We surf the waves of our thoughts as best we can, and try not to hold them back, or get overwhelmed. There is a sense of being alive. We can perform better in whatever we do.

This sense of aliveness will not come about miraculously. We need to invest some time in mind, body and relationships, to learn new strategies for mindful living. It is essentially a journey of self-discovery. Too many people sleepwalk through life in varying degrees of pain and suffering and never look within. They never take the opportunity to fully understand what their contribution might be, beyond fear.

Committing to mindfulness is not to obsess on a challenge or to navel gaze in your comfort zone, but to recognise what serves you best. In doing this you learn to state your intentions.

You learn to focus in a balanced way. You learn to play with the best tool in your toolkit: your attitude. You learn to be more mindful.

Mindful living and walking can get you closer to the peace, health and well-being you deserve.

AN AIDE-MEMOIRE FOR MINDFUL WALKING

Mindfulness is not a reclusive, monastic practise removed from your world of life and work. Not everyone has the desire or indeed the opportunity to take themselves off to a monastery.

Mindfulness is not about switching off from the world or avoiding people in it. It does not have time for being angry or resentful or anxious about the world or yourself. It is about using your on-board mind / brain / body computer in an emotionally intelligent way and to best effect. With this you can at every sensory level experience the world in front of your nose.

The breath is the most elegant tool in your toolbox; it is the whetstone that sharpens other tools. It is the key to knowing the workings of your own mind beyond the intellectual understanding that psychology or any other science might give you. To focus on the breath, that powerful, life-giving force, is to come home at times to a childlike simplicity, to inspire yourself literally and metaphorically to a way that is authentic for you.

The attitude you take to your breath is the other key. The seven pillars of mindfulness – Non-Judging, Patience, Beginner's Mind, Trust, Non-Striving, Acceptance and Letting Go – guide the way in this respect. An attitude of openness to all experience, and a profound curiosity about it beyond any judging, brings mind, body and spirit together in a way that can unlock your potential to be as you are. This is a place of much deeper awareness and knowing. It is a place of authenticity beyond any need to defend. You are your true self beyond the many masks you might have worn over time.

This is a place where doing and being melt into one. They make sense. The positive emotions of exhilaration, passion, joy, love, care, kindness, appreciation, gratitude and harmony sit with inner peace, equanimity, acceptance, forgiveness, serenity, reflection and contentment.

The alternative could be a toxic place of frustration, anger, hostility, fear, worry, anxiety, guilt, shame, resentment, judgement, hopelessness, despair, depression, burnout, fatigue, withdrawal, boredom and apathy.

Words do really have personalities. Mindful Walking offers you a choice. There is always choice and a better way of doing. Mindful Walking allows you just to be, in motion.

Living and performing effectively is about developing the skills that are likely to work best. Positive psychological skills such as visualisation and goal setting, allied to mindfulness skills, offer choice and the best way forward to peace, health and well-being. This is a combination of physical and mental doing and being. It is a physical and emotional fitness regime for you.

WHAT NEXT

- Make it your intention to set aside some time today to slow down, STOP and just be. Listen to the silence.

Create time to practise mindfulness, either lying or sitting.

- Observe your thinking, emotions and behaviours. You are not your thoughts. Don't believe everything you think.

- Learn not to 'take the bait' of every challenge that presents. Don't get caught or hooked on the first reaction you have in any situation. Try not to get onto every bus that passes your bus stop. They are only thoughts and emotions. They all pass.

- Explore your own style. What is recurring for you? What might be holding you back? What do you need to let go of?

- Savour this quiet time for yourself with a mindset of gratitude. It is a time to be easy and compassionate with yourself. It is a time to replenish your energy before you engage with the world of doing again. For this time there is no war to be fought or struggle to engage in. All is ok.

- Build mindfulness into all your activities today. Do them more mindfully.

    - Observe your thinking, emotions, feelings and behaviours. Where are you now in this moment of doing? What are you noticing? What are you noticing that is different?

    - Come back to your breath regularly. Use each new breath and activity as an opportunity to practise, especially when you might sense stress in your body. Don't forget the socially acceptable deep breath. This is just the next breath that you deliberately choose to observe as it fills your lungs and then recedes naturally. Just one breath can bring you back to a calmer place.

- Slow down. Savour. Smell the coffee. Do what you enjoy more mindfully throughout the day. Create the intention to be in the moment more often. Savour that piece of chocolate in all its intensity and flavour and pleasure. Observe what you are thinking and feeling. You may find that you don't need to shove another piece into your mouth so readily. Get your hands muddy in the earth. Do something completely different. Have fun.

- In all of your doing, be aware of your attitude. Does it focus on the 'Why' or negative aspects in me?

- As best you can and throughout the day, focus on the 'How.' Look for solutions, talk solutions, and think solutions. Problems are platforms for solutions. Develop new choices. There is a better way of viewing and doing.

- Wherever you find yourself, walk in mindful steps, every day. Try and develop both formal and informal walking practise every day. It might be a mindful walk across to your bedroom window before you start your day, or a mindful walk to the car as you go to work, or a mindful stroll during your lunch break, or a long, mindful walk when you get home in the evening. Take fresh air. Enjoy the light and the sunlight.

- Sleep well.

• Be mindful of relationships.

- Much psychological research suggests that the single biggest factor determining our happiness is relationships. While aloneness has its benefits, too much of it can be lonely, or painful. This is what the reality of losing a partner or friend is like. Mindfulness helps us to develop the capacity to be comfortable, alone in our own company. Relationships are about belonging and feeling safe.

- Participate in some activity beyond the self. Where that is not work, find some other way to participate and make a contribution. Get your friends to walk with you today. Volunteer to organise the walk. If no one comes, go alone – they might join you next time.

- Take inspiration from the least likely people. Johnny Barnes simply shows up to work every day with a positive attitude. He has created his own work. Nobody gave him a job. He is dependable and just wishes people well. How simple is that.

The paradox of mindfulness is that we do not set out to get anywhere on this journey, or control anything. It is what the title of the Jon Kabat-Zinn book teaches: *Wherever You Go, There You Are.* You just need to develop a mindset in which to be present is to be where you are at this very moment.

On the walk, on the journey, we focus our attention. We just notice and observe, non-judgementally, and let it go, whatever it is, either good or bad.

Two questions have travelled with us over the course of this book, and I hope you'll take them home as a keepsake to look back on from time to time.

1. What attachments are weighing me down, and holding me back? What am I carrying in the rucksack of my life that is unnecessary for the journey?

2. In order to enjoy a fuller, less anxious, lighter experience on the walk of life, what do I need to let go of? How can I lighten the load?

You are the only one who can answer these questions for yourself at this juncture. In answering these questions, the entire journey will be a lighter place of 'being', not mindless, distorted negative 'doing.' The thinking, judging mind, which anticipates things that may never happen, will not be running the show.

In taking a more mindful approach, you will tap the unique energy that is your essence and potential, beyond outside interference. Your performance will improve, but always remember: life inevitably does not turn out the way we planned it. Compassion for yourself and for others in a mindful approach will be needed more than ever then. Until the walk ends and we are forced to let go, there is always another hill around the corner. Why not walk up that hill mindfully, notice the colours and smells and make it easier and more enjoyable for yourself and others.

There are forces at work, unique for each of us, which can positively and negatively impact on our performance at any moment in our lives. With mindfulness, we can walk these forces off, the good and the bad, and reach equilibrium.

You might have a sense that this is the end. It is really only the beginning. Good luck with the rest of your walk as it flourishes into a journey. Perhaps we may meet on the walk or even on the 'Paps' on the next winter solstice. Go peacefully and in curiosity because I'm off now to mindfully walk the length and breadth of the country. I hope we'll cross paths along the way.

BIBLIOGRAPHY

Chaskalson, M. (2011) *The Mindful Workplace: Developing Resilient Individuals and Resonant Organisations with MBSR*. London: Wiley Blackwell

Collins, J. (2001) *Good to Great*. New York: Harper Collins

Crane, R. (2009) *Mindfulness-Based Cognitive Therapy*. New York: Routledge

Fletcher, A. (2001) *The Art of Looking Sideways*. London: Phaidon Press

Gallwey, W.T. (2000) *The Inner Game of Work: Focus, Learning, Pleasure and Mobility in the Workplace*. New York: Random House

Gardner, F.L. and Moore, Z.E. (2007) *The Psychology of Enhancing Human Performance: The Mindfulness-Acceptance-Commitment (MAC) Approach*. New York: Springer

Hanson, R. and Mendius, R. (2009) *Buddha's Brain: Happiness, Love and Wisdom*. Oakland, CA: New Harbinger Publications

Kabat-Zinn, J. (1996). *Full Catastrophe Living: How to cope with stress, pain and illness using mindfulness meditation.* London: Piatkus

Kabat-Zinn, J. (2009) *Wherever You Go, There You Are: Mindfulness Meditation in Everyday Life*. New York: Hyperion

Kahneman, D. (2011) *Thinking, Fast and Slow.* London: Penguin

Killingsworth, M.A and Gilbert, D.T. (2010) 'A Wandering Mind is an Unhappy Mind' *Science*

Macfarlane, R,. (2003) *Mountains of the mind: A history of fascination.* London: Granta books

Menon, D. (2009) *Stop Sleepwalking Through Life: 9 Lessons To Increase Your Awareness.* Mumbai: Yogi Impressions Books

Mental Health Foundation (UK) (2010) 'Be Mindful' report. www.mentalhealth.org/publications/be-mindful-report

Murphy, D. (2003) *Eight Feet in the Andes: Travels with a Mule in Unknown Peru.* London: John Murray

Robbins, A. 'Leaders create breakthroughs: The three mandates of Leadership.' http://training.tonyrobbins.com/leaders-create-breakthroughs-the-three-mandates-of-leadership/

Scott, S. (2002) *Fierce Conversations: Achieving Success in Work and in Life, One Conversation at a Time.* London: Piatkus

Hanh, T.N. (2008) *The Miracle of Mindfulness.* London: Random House

Tolle, E. (1997) *The Power of Now.* New York: Hodder Mobius

Williams, M. and Penman, D. (2011) *Mindfulness:*

A Practical Guide to Finding Peace in a Frantic World.
London: Piatkus

Whitmore, J. (2002) *Coaching for Performance: Growing People, Performance and Purpose.* London: Nicholas Brealey Publishing

ACKNOWLEDGEMENTS

This book is the result of a long journey and a lot of walking and talking with some wonderful people over four decades. This walking hasn't always been easy. I have not gotten to the top of every summit, but whether up hill, down dale, and in some wonderful places and spaces that I have walked around the world, it has always been about the people I met and the people who travelled with me. They are the special people who guided and supported me throughout.

Little was I to know in my last year in school that when a former teacher of mine, Eamon Young, took me and 31 other energetic students on our first hill walk that it would be the first dot of walking experience and the start of a lifetime love of walking experiences. He was a teacher and ex-army man himself. On that day when we disembarked chaotically from our bus on the side of the road, he divided our group into three sections of ten and put one person from each section in charge of their own section. I was left standing around without a role until he told me that I was in charge of the lot for the day.

Although I didn't fully appreciate it at the time, this was my first introduction to a military career for which I am truly grateful. I must thank my colleagues and friends from the Irish Defence Forces for their friendship and the formative learning I received when I needed it most. My interest in human performance and my own in particular, good and bad, emerged both at home and abroad over 23 years in this wonderful force which truly practises the value of service. More young men and women should be given the opportunity to learn in this unique Irish university of life and peaceful service.

I would like to specifically thank Dick Murtagh, my friend and former colleague of those forty years. He was with me when I first started out in the Defence Forces. Since then he has travelled and walked with me at home and abroad and provided much sound comment and advice, especially with regard to the Camino de Santiago which he regularly walks. In this regard I must also acknowledge the insights and guidance on the Camino provided by Cathy Kiernan O'Connell from Edinburgh. My friend the Sergeant Major (Retd) from Tralee,

Ted Moynihan, is regularly the source of wise commentary and not just associated with walking.

To those wonderful companions who have walked with me over the years in the Andes, Himalayas, Russia, Africa and around Europe and at home, this book is a testament to the learning I gained through walking and talking. The Tánaiste ('Deputy' in Irish) on those walks, Anthony O'Donovan, deserves special mention. Organising groups is not easy and more especially in the busy airports we transited on our way around the world. He was never found wanting even when the mindful attention and focus of some group members was less than was required.

To Tim, Adrian, Sarah, Frank and Sinead who shared their own stories of mindfulness and mindful walking in this book, I salute and thank you all. You are an inspiration to us.

To my colleague in University College Cork, Pat O'Leary, I extend special thanks for his part on this journey. On workshops associated with programmes that we both have developed and run in the university, the central pillars of self-coaching, positive psychology, emotional intelligence and mindfulness have been discussed and refined to present my current best understanding of mindful walking and its practise. It is a marriage made somewhere. I question his evidence and he questions my faith.

For his energy and enthusiasm and support, I am indebted to Professor Stephen Palmer, a thought leader in the domain of Coaching Psychology. He provided the space, opportunity and encouragement for me to develop my own understanding of this process we call coaching and the positive psychology underpinning it. Psychology is really only about a scientific understanding of how the mind works in our efforts to make sense of the world. Mindfulness and mindful walking is about a better way of making sense of that world.

Fortunate strokes of serendipity are rare. It was my good fortune to ask a simple question of David Corkery, the former Irish International rugby player, when it appeared to me to be needed. What followed that question is this book and a conversation which I hope continues long into the future. He is a generous man with an enormous heart. He opened the door to a series of events which I could not have predicted. Such is life if you ask questions and share a meaningful conversation.

It was also my good fortune to ask Wally Quirke to capture mindful walking in a sketch / motif. I am so glad I did.

I would like to thank all the people of Hachette Ireland for their wonderful support throughout the writing of this book. A special thanks to the two Ciaras, Considine and Doorley. Their positivity was a tremendous support to me when I was most in doubt. Also to Maggie Armstrong who pointed out the error of my thinking and ways in the kindest and most patient fashion as the book took final shape.

I wish to thank my wonderful and loving mother and father, Maeve and Vincent, who are no longer with us, but who gave me and my four sisters, Clair, Ursula, Maeve and Orla, the power, energy and curiosity to step outside our comfort zones from time to time.

To my two beautiful daughters, Aoife and Jean, I must extend a special loving embrace of thanks. You are both a joy and you continue to teach me beyond anything you fully appreciate yourselves at this time.

And finally, to my friend, my partner, my rock, my wife Michele, who I must thank for her enduring patience and belief in me when the clouds were darkest. Writing this book has been the best year of my life. It would not have happened without her. To her I dedicate this book.

PERMISSIONS